One Waaf's War

One Waaf's War

Joan Beech

British Library Cataloguing in Publication Data

Beech, Joan

For data please refer to publisher

ISBN 0 7104 3063 9

First published in Great Britain 1989

 Enquiries to:
D J Costello (Publishers) Ltd
43 The High Street
Tunbridge Wells
Kent TN1 1XL

Typeset in 11 on 13pt Century Schoolbook by
Litho Link Limited, Welshpool, Powys
Printed by Billings and Sons Ltd, Worcester

Contents

Foreword

While I was writing this book, friends would ask, 'Why have you waited forty years before putting it all down on paper?'

Why indeed?

At the end of World War 2 when we were all finally demobilised, we had had enough of war and uniforms, rules and regulations, and only wanted to get on with our interrupted private lives. After I came out of the Waaf, I didn't think much about my Service life, being too busy getting on with the present. In common with a lot of my contemporaries, I regarded the war as having taken six years out of my life – six years wasted in many ways. I have come to see that this is a wrong point of view, that all experience has its worth and its place in the scheme of things. But for years after the war ended the world still appeared to be in a state of turmoil, and I'm sure I was not the only one to wonder what had been the purpose of it all, except perhaps to snuff out a lot of promising young lives.

Then suddenly it was 1984, and in June the 40th anniversary of D-Day was coming up. A lot was said and written about this event in the newspapers and on radio and TV, and people were asked to write to the BBC about their memories of that time, the accounts to be incorporated in a radio programme on or near the date of June 6th.

I sat back and thought about it and decided that I might have something to contribute. After all, there couldn't be that number of women still living in the UK who knew before it was announced by the BBC on the morning of June 6th that the invasion of Europe had started, except for those who were actually involved in it. Being a very junior member of Bomber Command, I was not involved in the organisation of the invasion, but I certainly knew before the majority of the population that it was at last under way.

I began to write and once started, the memories came flooding back. Before I knew where I was, the brief account was turning into a full length book. It seemed I did have something to say which might be of interest to those who were old enough to remember the war, and perhaps also to many of the younger generation who do now appear to want to know about these events which happened before they were born, and which changed the course of history.

When I had finished the first draft, the late Air Vice Marshal Donald Bennett, who was in charge of the Pathfinder group of Bomber Command during the war, was good enough to read it, and his comments greatly encouraged me. He wrote, 'Thank you for letting me read your "One Waaf's War". Pure nostalgia! Congratulations!' He was an elderly man at that time and probably not in the best of health, but I am ever grateful for his remarks. At that point I hadn't even thought of a title for the book, but here was one ready made.

Recently, a younger friend of mine read the book and said to me, a trifle wistfully, that she wished she was a few years older and could have been a Waaf during the war, as she feels she was born too late and missed it all!

Well, that's one point of view, I suppose. I do find that having written down all I can remember, the things that stay in my mind are not so much the disasters and tragedies that occurred, but the happier occasions, the many different people that I met and the good times we had together.

I hope that any ex-Waafs of Bomber Command who happen to read my version of the events of the war years will recall their own days in uniform, and perhaps feel as I now do that it was, with all its trials and anxieties and plain hard work, a time worth living through.

Joan Beech
Victoria, Canada
March 1989

1

Aircraftwoman Second Class

It was the beginning of January 1943, in the middle of World War II, and things were not going well for the Allies. Ever since Pearl Harbour and the sinking of the warships *Repulse* and *Prince of Wales* in December 1941, news of disasters had been coming in thick and fast from all over the globe, from the retreat of the British 8th Army in North Africa to the US Army surrendering on Bataan in the Pacific. Allied shipping losses from U-boats in the Atlantic were at a constantly high level, threatening our food supplies; the island of Malta was enduring a month long siege and its people were almost starving; the Naval convoys on the Murmansk run continued to endure appalling weather and conditions, and the battle for Stalingrad went on and on. And in February 1942, there was the loss of Singapore with 85,000 troops and civilians either killed or taken prisoner. Somewhere in there the Americans won the Battle of Midway in the Pacific, but at the time its significance was not realised amongst this welter of bad news. Look where you liked, all seemed to be dark and hopeless. I think the lowest point for the people of Britain was the loss of Singapore, the so-called impregnable fortress. It was incredible, unthinkable – but it happened.

By the middle of 1942 British troops were active all round the world in the many different theatres of war, and the manpower shortage in England was becoming acute. At this point a decision was made at government level to start conscripting women to take the place of men in the Forces in certain non-combatant jobs, so that yet more men could be spared to go overseas. The Women's Forces had of course been recruiting volunteers since the start of the war, but for many like myself who were working in what were known as 'reserved occupations', it was not possible to volunteer, no matter how badly we might want to. I was a shorthand-typist working in one of the Railway Executive Headquarters offices in North London, and was given to understand that this was work of 'National Importance'. I was certainly informed that I could not change my job for the duration of the war, so therefore it came as a great shock when a government decision was made to release for call-up one age group of girls in reserved jobs. And this age group happened to be mine.

My calling-up papers for the Women's Auxillary Air Force arrived with impeccable timing on Christmas Day 1942, and caused much tearing of hair and gnashing of teeth amongst my nearest and dearest, notably my mother, who took it as a personal affront that her one and only daughter should be torn from the bosom of her family and sent miles away from home, to meet and mix with all manner of people – and 'foreigners as well, probably.'

She had my future all nicely mapped out. Three doors down the road from our house lived Cedric, who was two years older than me, incredibly handsome, a wow with all the girls, and a navigator on heavy bombers in the RAF. I had known him for as long as I could remember and he got on well with my parents, as well as being like an older brother to me – the older brother I had always wanted but never had. More importantly, he was single and the only son of comfortably-off parents. I know my mother had high hopes that before long Cedric's roving eye would light on me, and he would realise in a blinding flash that I had grown up while he had been away attending to the war. Then would come the formal engagement, followed by a white wedding, and we would start married life in a nice little house just around the corner and within easy reach of her maternal ministrations. Alas for her hopes and dreams! They all crashed into ruins on the night of October 15th 1942, when he and his plane disappeared without trace on a night bomber raid over Germany. He was reported missing for a time, then 'missing, believed killed', which was the official wording for those whose bodies were never found, who were either blown to bits in the air or who crashed into the sea. I wasn't in love with him, but all the same it was a very sad time, especially for his grieving parents. All I could think of was, what a waste, what a terrible waste!

For a long time I felt sure he was not dead, that somehow he had survived and would eventually find his way back to England. He was fluent in French and Spanish and I pictured him hiding out in some peasant's house, then being smuggled out in a fishing boat and finally turning up on our doorstep, grinning and in rags but very much alive. It never happened. No trace of him or his crew was ever found, which makes me think his aircraft did go down in the North Sea.

Apart from the tragedy of Cedric's disappearance, I couldn't help but feel that at this time I was becoming a grave disappointment to my mother. I realised that it was a daughter's first duty once she reached her early twenties to get married, preferably to someone well-heeled and good-looking, and certainly a good nine months before the appearance of the first grand-child. But I did seem to have missed the bus. Most of the girls I was at school with had already had their walk down the aisle with the man of their choice, some of them with what appeared to me to be indecent haste, and quite a few were already pushing prams around the north London suburb where we lived. The outbreak of war was a signal for large numbers of girls of my age to flock to the Parish Church to tie the knot with current boyfriends, and most Saturday afternoons saw at least one white wedding at St Mary's Church. No-one looked very far ahead. We did after all expect to be bombed out of existence from the time we heard the first air-raid siren a few minutes after Mr Chamberlain made his sad, historic radio announcement that this country was now at war with Germany. The boys of my age group at school were among the first to get called up under the Conscription Act, and by the time the war had been on for two years, at least three of those I had been friendly with had already been killed, and two others were prisoners-of-war in Germany, one of them since Dunkirk. I had never been in any mad hurry to get married, and when I saw the men, or boys, that some of the girls were marrying, I wasn't sure that I wanted to get married at all.

Only the other day I had come face to face with one of my girlfriends from school days, one Mabel Mumford. Mabel was 5ft tall, with thick pebble glasses and halitosis, and she was leading by the hand an unprepossessing youth with floppy hair and the same kind of glasses. He may have had the other problem too, but I didn't get close enough to find out. For some inexplicable reason they were both wearing tartan kilts, his coming down well below his knees, and as he was only an inch or two taller than Mabel, he didn't cut a very dashing figure. He was introduced bashfully as 'my fiancé', and I was able to wish them both the best of luck without any feelings of envy. I mean, he may have had a lovely nature, but it didn't add up to Romance as depicted on the cinema screen by Fred Astaire and Ginger Rogers, and I felt I would sooner remain single than be married to someone who looked like that, thank you.

I couldn't, however, expect my mother to understand all this. She had been walking out with my father since they were both sixteen, and neither of them had ever looked at anyone else. I didn't seem to be coming up to scratch at all, so, the atmosphere at home being somewhat dismal, I was not sorry for a change of scene, and I was glad that it was the Waaf I was going to join, because of Cedric.

So there I was at Euston Station in London, along with hundreds of other girls, under the great echoing canopy of the station roof, watching a train backing slowly into Platform 1. This train had been laid on for us alone, and we all stood watching quietly. We had been chattering away like starlings, but now our future was sliding quietly to a halt in front of us, and apprehension silenced our tongues. Whatever happened next, whatever was in store for us, it was bound to be an entirely different life from anything we had hitherto experienced and beyond our powers to visualise. We climbed in, eight to a compartment, and set out into the unknown, which turned out to be the main recruitment camp at Gloucester.

At that time the Waaf was taking in over 1,000 recruits a week and, when you think about it, this was quite some operation. All these girls had to be fed, clothed, drilled, taught a trade, and then thrust willy-nilly into the war machine, no matter what other private plans they may have had for themselves over the next few months. It didn't take us long to realise that our private lives would from now on be pushed very much into the background for the duration of the war.

In the railway compartment I sat next to a very pretty girl called Dulcie Barker, who couldn't sound her rrr's and was most put out at this disruption of her life, as she was going to be 'mawwied' next month. Another little girl, Betty, having been seen off by a devoted, middle-aged father, spent the first part of the journey in tears. Dulcie kept smiling at her very kindly and in fact this was the beginning of a friendship between them. Not many of us had ever been away from home before and we were in the main children of middle-class parents. We came from nice, comfortable homes and had never had to rough it, but we soon found out that we had left our cosy nests behind us for the foreseeable future.

We were five days at Gloucester, living in Nissen huts while we had a series of inoculations, our first instructions in drilling, and were kitted out in our uniforms. Five days! – it seemed like five years. So many different impressions crowded in on us, so many different instructions issued from different females in blue uniforms, that I for one was totally bewildered. My main impression, looking back, is of darkness, cold and damp. The huts were long and low, with beds arranged along both sides at right angles to the walls, an uncooperative cast-iron coke-burning stove in the centre which we had to contrive to light and keep going, hard blankets, and sheets which, judging by the dank feel of them had just had a rapid wash after the departure of the last intake of girls and were not yet properly dry. Shades of my house-proud mum, who would never have allowed a sheet anywhere near a bed unless it had been washed, dried, ironed and *then* aired!

We were given various small jobs to do, such as sweeping the floors in the huts and looking after the aforementioned coke stove, and one of my jobs was to scrub the floor of the small lobby inside the door of the hut. I am ashamed to say that I had never scrubbed a floor in my life, and although I did my best, the result was that the floor looked more murky than it had before – in fact the Waaf Officer who came to inspect it, accused me of not washing it at all.

Our uniforms, when first put on, looked dreadful – they were creased and stiff, and fitted where they touched, the only comfort being that we all looked as peculiar as each other. We seemed to spend hours lined up in squads outside on the parade ground, watching the snowflakes settling on each other's caps, standing to attention and then at ease, getting colder and more miserable all the time.

There was, however, one Waaf Sergeant whom we really liked. She smiled at us and made us jump up and down to keep warm, do running on the spot and slap our knees with our hands to keep the circulation going. One felt she hadn't forgotten what it was like to be a raw recruit and homesick. I noticed she wore a big diamond and sapphire ring on her engagement finger, and one day when we were all standing in line in front of her, waiting for something, I know not what, to happen, she furtively whipped a letter out of her pocket and started to read it – we all decided it was from her fiancé and we wondered if he was also in the Air Force.

We had to line up (indoors) for our inoculations against typhoid and tetanus, and vaccinations against smallpox. A few weak souls collapsed and had to be carted away, and of course it wasn't pleasant. Then we were given 24 hours off to recover, and we certainly needed this – the typhoid jab gave us all high temperatures. By the time our five days were up, most of us had streaming colds and hacking coughs, but one final horror was in store – FFI (free from infection) physical examination. Here we were all paraded in a hall, wearing only bras and pants, and had to present ourselves before a Waaf doctor, removing our pants as we did so. I only had a vague idea what she could be looking for, but it was one final indignity which caused us all to steam with embarrassment.

In retrospect I realise that in fact the whole business of introducing girls in their thousands into the Armed Forces (a move unprecedented in Britain's history) was conducted with great speed and efficiency, and couldn't have been organised any better if it had been planned for centuries. We had to shut our minds to the fact that we were all known by a number and a surname, and had to conform at least outwardly to a certain rigid standard. No little individualistic touches could be added to our uniforms. Caps had to be worn straight, the brass buttons of our coats to be polished to a shine fit to dazzle the onlooker, and sexless black lace-up shoes attempted to make all shapes and sizes of feet look like boats. Here, however, I did produce a slight deviation from the accepted norm. I am blessed (or cursed) with a very high instep, and after a few months of battling with the regulation shoes, the latter began to resemble Dutch clogs, with the toes permanently turned up. You could always pick out my shoes in any line up of Waaf shoes, with or without feet in them.

Later on I met a Waaf who had a similar problem and I was extremely put out to find that as she had been a dancer (ie, chorus girl) in civilian life and also had thin feet with a high instep, she was allowed to have her Waaf shoes *specially made!* So what? I thought indignantly. I suppose as I was only a typist my feet were reckoned to be as flat as barges. For the three and a half years I was in uniform, my shoes always looked odd, no matter how often I polished them or put shoe trees in them, and in the end I just lost interest in my feet.

The few days at Gloucester allowed us a bit of time to get to know each other, and we began to get ourselves sorted out into the different trades we were going to enter – cooks, telephonists, clerks, transport drivers, nursing orderlies, etc. I was bound for the Meteorological Office when trained, and before long had found another prospective Met Assistant, one Jackie Ross-Evans, who cottoned on to me with great zest, exclaiming, 'Hooray! Let's stick together!' When I had had a good look at her I made up my mind to stay as far away from her as possible. She was a type I had never met before and in my ignorance I thought she was mad. She was tall, angular, with an outrageous 'county' accent which I thought was put on (it wasn't), and was wearing a hat with a three foot long feather. What problems she had when we had to parcel up our civilian clothes to send them home! There was no way that feather would go into any parcel and I wondered how anyone could be so stupid as to wear a thing like that to join the Waaf in.

Then the time came for us to leave the initial training camp and make room for the next intake. So, wearing our ill-fitting uniforms and with a small wrapped package of lunch dangling from one of the buttons of our greatcoats (thus leaving our hands free to cope with kitbags and hats), we left by train again, this time for Morecambe in Lancashire. This was a long and tortuous journey, involving several stops and much shunting about, and we were warned not to attempt to leave the train. What if someone had? Would she have been shot through the knees as she weaved her way across tracks and behind trucks? To my knowledge no-one ever attempted this desperate venture. I think we already knew the system could not be beaten.

The arrival in Morecambe is something eternally engraved on my memory. Picture the scene – a large, shadowy platform and a thousand girls with kitbags pouring out of the train, not knowing what to do next and mostly feeling lost and tired. We were met by a tall, blonde Waaf Flight Sergeant who proceeded to shriek and bully us into arranging ourselves in alphabetical order in front of her and separating off into groups according to the first letter of our surnames, so that most of us found ourselves amongst strangers again. I reflected that if this was service life, I didn't think I was going to like it. In depressed silence we got ourselves sorted out and were marched off in batches to our billets. We were all billeted in peacetime holiday boarding houses, run by slightly resentful landladies who soon informed us that they much preferred to accommodate the boys in the RAF, and weren't at all keen on taking girls.

However, once we were settled I think most of us enjoyed our three weeks in Morecambe. We were there primarily to be instructed in drilling, or 'square bashing'. Apparently the war could not proceed satisfactorily unless we all knew how to march in step, to halt, turn right and left and about turn without tripping over our feet. Inevitably, there was the odd one in each squad who didn't know left from right, but generally speaking it was pleasant enough – three weeks of outdoor training in the crisp pure air. The corporal in charge of my squad was extremely smart herself, and was always exhorting us to further efforts, as she said there was a squad up the other end of the promenade who were *very good!* Sure enough, we marched up there one day and there was a 'B' squad doing its stuff. There was no doubt about how good they were – all in step, arms swinging up to the shoulder in unison and Dulcie Barker looking grim, with her hat rammed down to her ears, intent on being the smartest Waaf of them all.

It took a few weeks for us to become accustomed to wearing a uniform. Not many of us had, since we stopped being Guides and Brownies. I for one had never worn a proper shirt and tie before, and after a very short while I began to sympathise with men who had to wear these things all the time. Ties were bad enough but the shirt collar rubbed my neck and made it sore. And whoever it was thought up the style of the Airwoman's hat must have had a strong grudge against women, it was so unflattering. Still, there we were, with our civilian clothes all parcelled up and on their way home, so we had, perforce, to make the best of things. The greatcoat which we all had to wear in the winter appeared to be designed for six foot models, and as soon as we arrived in Morecombe there was a concerted rush round to a local tailor to have the bottom six inches or so lopped off. He could hardly have made a fortune, shortening Waaf skirts at five bob a time, but it made such a difference to our morale. My coat originally came right down to my ankles and made me look a freak. Not for the first time I envied the tall, slim girls who looked so much better in their uniforms than we shorties.

After a week or two I even got the hang of tying that tie and no longer had to watch myself in a mirror, doing it the wrong way round. But I was very much piqued when a few weeks later I went home and met a former boyfriend, who made a sneering remark within my hearing that you could always pick out the rookie Waafs by the duff knots in their ties. If he had observed us a little more closely he would have noticed an even surer sign of newness, the bright yellow of our brass buttons, which took months of daily polishing before they began to approximate the mellow, liquid shine that spoke of years of service. I told myself he was just jealous. He was still a civilian, a sheet-metal worker in some factory in north London and had managed to get his call-up deferred. The very fact of being in uniform, however raw-looking, gave me a feeling of superiority over civilians, who were still battling with clothing coupons and had to endlessly make-do-and-mend.

Back in Morecambe, when we were not drilling our time was entirely taken up in variety of other ways. We were never left with time to sit and think – or perhaps we might have sat and wondered what on earth we were doing up there. In the evenings we had everlasting buttons to polish and shoes to clean, undies to wash and baths to queue up for in turn, and in the daytime we were required to attend lectures, go on not-too-exhausting little route marches, and learn the social structure of life as a Waaf.

To take the last first – this structure was quite simple really. You entered on the bottom rung of the ladder as an Aircraftwoman 2nd Class, which meant there was nobody lower than you, and almost everyone you met who had a stripe on her sleeve could tell you what to do and where to go – and usually did. The next step up was Aircraftwoman 1st Class, and then Leading Aircraftwoman when you were allowed to have a felt propellor sewn onto the sleeves of your uniform jacket, and this you were awarded when you were considered proficient in your particular trade. Corporals came next – two stripes halfway up the arms. Our squad was lucky as we had Corporal Flint, who was pretty and smart and very kind to us. Next came the Sergeants, three stripers, and I remember one called Sergeant Hill, only a young girl, probably younger than me, with a voice loud enough to fill the Albert Hall, who drove us unmercifully in her efforts to smarten up this bunch of wet lettuces she had been landed with. Continuing up the ranks we come to Flight Sergeants (three stripes and a crown) – we only had one of these, the one who had greeted us on our arrival, and wasn't that enough? Lastly, Waaf Officers. These had better-cut uniforms than ours, of superior material, thinner stockings and not quite such hideous hats. They had to be called 'Ma'am' like Royalty, and were to be saluted whenever we met face to face with our hats on. It was impressed upon us in the very early days that you never saluted without your hat on, the reason being (so we were told) that the salute dated back to the knights of old who wore visors with their armour and had to raise their visors in order to speak to people, and this developed into the modern salute as we know it. Since my Waaf days I have seen countless films of American soldiers, sailors and airmen saluting like mad without their hats on, but of course they don't have much history. Anyway, I was always in trouble in Morecombe for committing the sin of walking past officers (hats on), without saluting, mainly because I just didn't see them, and then would have to be called and reprimanded, to the great edification of passers-by. I must admit I did resent all these rules and the authority which seemed to weigh us down. After all, I had had quite a reasonable job in civilian life, with a fair amount of authority of my own, and here I was being treated like the village idiot at times. Those girls who volunteered for the Services straight from school had an easier time of it, as they were used to being told what to do.

Saluting was a bit of a problem, not only remembering to do it, but doing it properly. We had to practice in front of a mirror – right arm out straight, smartly up to hit the cap badge and then stiffly down, all to the count of four. When we went on Pay Parade to collect our pittance, once every two weeks, we had to assemble in a hall, our names would be read out alphabetically (hard luck if you were near the end), then up we would go to the pay table, reel off name and last three figures of our number, salute the Paying Officer with the right arm, scoop up the money with the left hand, about turn and march out. I always felt a complete idiot doing this and was sure that the epithet 'wet lettuce' was coined solely to describe people like me, who were not the right shape to enhance the severity of a military uniform. I probably looked limp all over and certainly felt it as I crept out, clutching the hard-earned cash in my hot, wet hand.

The lectures were on such rivetting subjects as Hygiene and First Aid and the History of the RAF. Once we were harangued for forty-five minutes by a terrifying woman who had evidently been in the Waaf forever judging by the number of medal ribbons she wore, and who appeared to be wearing her uniform over a body of ultra-stiff cardboard. Her astonishing message was, 'Girls, do not go out with American servicemen, as some of them have Negro blood in them and it doesn't always *show*. You could end up with *black babies*!' A fair proportion of us, including myself, were not only virginal but ignorant with it, and we just couldn't understand what she could *mean*! She so scared me that for months afterwards if I saw an American soldier I would look sideways at him, trying to assess the possibilities of black ancestors, and this led to a few highly embarrassing encounters, I can tell you.

On one other occasion, a young Pilot Officer of the RAF, in a uniform which looked almost as new as ours, had to deliver to us a lecture on classical music. On looking back, this does seem rather a waste of time as he had no musical instrument with him to illustrate the points he was trying to make, and surely a talk about music without hearing any of it can only be of interest to someone who knows a bit about it. A large percentage of his captive audience were obviously bored silly, and some who didn't have the good manners to try to hide their disinterest started to play cards at the back of the hall. The Waaf officers and NCOs on view didn't seem to be very concerned at this behaviour. I suppose to them it was just one more way of keeping all these girls occupied for an afternoon. But I felt very sorry for the poor young man – he must have known he hadn't got through to many of us.

There was only one route march on our schedule and this we approached with some trepidation, having visions of a 50 mile hard slog carrying our kitbags and arriving back exhausted, with bleeding feet, or perhaps even on a stetcher. But no, it was nothing like that. We were marched briskly (minus kitbags), a squad at a time, round a few corners and out onto the edge of the open country, with a sergeant and a corporal leading, another corporal bringing up the rear and the rest of us more or less in step in the middle. It was a lovely day for January; the sun shone and everywhere looked crisp and clean under a light frost. When we had gone far enough to work up a mild perspiration, we were halted in a country lane and told to stand at ease. Well, that was simple enough. After a week or two of continous drilling, there are only two ways you can stand – to attention or at ease. The NCOs then got their heads together, lit up cigarettes and proceeded to ignore us completely for the next half an hour, chatting amongst themselves. We didn't know what to make of this at all and there was much muttering and fidgeting in the ranks, while we shot suspicious glances at them and debated whether to make a run for it. Eventually the chat show broke up, we were called to order and marched at the same brisk pace back to base. And that was our route march.

We were lucky to have three weeks of good weather, for the middle of winter, and the invigorating air and outdoor life made me personally feel on top of the world. On one fresh, sunny afternoon when somehow I managed to get out for a walk all by myself, I saw for the first time the mountains of the Lake District clearly revealed across the bay. Since then I have travelled widely and seen plenty of real mountains (by which I mean *higher* mountains), but I still clearly remember the impact of those distant white-topped hills seen across the sparkling blue water, and beneath a cloudless blue sky. There can't be many views more beautiful than that.

Another afternoon I was walking back to my billet with J R Evans, who was sticking to me like glue, when we came upon an enterprising street photographer. He persuaded us to pose in front of a shop window for a snap 'to show the folks back home'. The resulting work of art (which I still have) shows two girls in uniform, standing to attention with their hats on dead straight, and simpering self-consciously in front of the display window of a gift shop. There on the windows were two large labels advertising the contents of the shop – the one immediately over my head said, 'leather goods', but over J R's head the label said, expressively, 'fancy goods'. I still wonder if the man arranged us like that on purpose.

This photographer was one of the few members of the male sex who were to be seen at all in Morecambe. One result of living in this almost entirely female environment was that when a man did appear, he drew every eye for miles around. 'A man!' we would shriek, rushing to the windows. Poor soul, he was most likely someone's husband or son or brother, home on leave from one of the Forces and hoping for a few days' peace and quiet, instead of which he must have wondered what had happened to his home town, with all these hundreds of blue females drilling on the promenade and overflowing from the boarding houses and hotels.

The landlady in the house where I was living had a son, an Able Seaman in the Royal Navy, and he happened to come home on leave while I was there. He was carefully inspected from over the banisters and pronounced to be 'not bad', and while most of us were too diffident to do more than say, 'good morning', when we passed in the hall, one of our number called Jenny, who was not the least bit bashful, manoeuvred herself a date with him. Later on she spent three hours sitting on the sofa with him (unknown to mother), finally creeping up to bed about 2am. 'That girl's asking for trouble,' he was heard to remark darkly to his mother the next morning, 'you mark my words!'

The only other man we saw was the fiancé of Molly who also lived in our house, and he got leave and came up to Morecambe especially to see her. She was a beautiful girl, with corn coloured hair and blue eyes and a natural peaches-and-cream complexion, and her fiancé Mark was a Canadian Flying Officer on a bomber aerodrome in East Anglia. He was due to arrive by train on a certain day and she went off happily to meet him, having been given the day off. Well, wartime trains were notoriously capricious in their departure and arrival times, and I don't think there was such a thing as a timetable, so poor Molly, after waiting at the station for ages, was approached by the RAF Police and marched ignominiously back to the billet, where she was confined to her room. They obviously thought she was trying to get away and, explain as she would, it cut no ice with the authorities. Luckily, Mark finally turned up, explained the situation, and Molly was duly released to meet him. Then she brought him home to meet all of us, the landlady produced a bottle of her home-made rhubarb wine, and we celebrated over the steak and kidney pie and rice pudding.

Shortly after this my three weeks was up. Most of the girls I met in Morecambe I never saw again, once we had dispersed to go on our various courses. Those like me who were destined for the Met Office did their two month's training in London, which was great for me, being a Londoner, and I left Lancashire at the beginning of February feeling fitter than I ever had before, and bound for 'the smoke'.

2

'They're all as dim as Toc H lamps'

We travelled down to London by train in the usual wartime discomfort. This train was not specially laid on for us as the previous ones had been, and when we changed at Crewe the one we got into was already full, so it was a case of cramming into the corridors and sitting on our kitbags.

Travelling by train during the war was always uncomfortable at best and this journey was a pretty average one – slow, cold and cramped. The train was three-quarters full of Service people, all en route from somewhere to somewhere, resigned but cheerful, and if anything was needed to put things into proportion for me, this journey was it. I was now part of a community, a band of brothers if you like (and sisters), uprooted from our homes and our settled, routine lives, and united by one common aim – to wipe Hitler off the map and get back home again. Of course, there were the Japs as well, but the Yanks could take care of them. We'd had our hands full since the middle of 1940 with Dunkirk, the Battle of Britain, the threatened invasion followed by the

Blitz and then two years of nothing but bad news, the only good news for us being that the USA had been dragged into the fight after Pearl Harbour. (Bad news for them, of course.) But I became aware for the first time of a united feeling; of not being alone any more. Wherever I went now in my blue uniform, I knew I would have friends to help me should I be in trouble. There was a community spirit among Service people which is perhaps accentuated in time of war when so many of us were only in it for the duration, and I felt glad to be a part of it.

There was only one thing worse than long distance day-time travel on the railways during wartime, and that was long distance night-time travel. The illumination in the carriages at night consisted of a small blue bulb in the ceiling because of the blackout, and that gave about enough light to peer into each other's faces but not enough to read by. You could either chat or go to sleep, while breathing in other people's cigarette smoke, and I've done enough of these journeys to know how boring and endless those nights could be. Sometimes the trains were so crowded that ten people would be squashed into the supposedly eight-seater compartments, with girls sitting on servicemens' knees, occasionally stretched out full length across the bodies, and sometimes even sleeping in the luggage racks and toilets. Then there was always the extra hazard when approaching a city of running into an air raid. Whenever this happened, trains tended to come to a halt altogether so as not to attract more attention than necessary from the intruders flying about overhead.

But this was an all-day trip and we arrived once again at Euston Station, at dusk, and were met by several RAF buses which ferried us quickly to our home for the next two months, a large block of flats near Victoria Station. There we were housed on the ninth floor and not allowed to use the lifts. Why this was I cannot remember but I expect there was a good reason. One thing was obvious – we were certainly going to keep fit, chasing up and down all those stairs.

We were not all Met Waafs. Trainees for several other trades were accommodated there, but mostly we stayed in our own little groups. It didn't take long to settle into a routine, and I didn't realise how unlike the usual run of Service life this was until two months later, when I was finally posted to an RAF bomber station. There were no morning or evening parades, and we travelled every day to a building in Oxford Street which used to be a department store and which had been requisitioned by the RAF for the purpose of our training. We were allowed to make our own way there by bus or train, the only proviso being that we had to be there by 9am each working day. Our evenings and weekends were free.

We knew we could be expected to be sent to RAF bomber stations in eastern England when we had completed our training, as this is where the action was at that stage of the war. Nearly every morning the BBC would announce over the radio that our aircraft had been out the night before over various targets in Germany or Italy, and all too often one or more of them failed to return. We were all very keen to complete our Met training in the shortest possible time so that we could be sent to where things were happening.

Meantime, we went back to school, taking instruction in geography and mathematics, learning the basics of weather interpretation and how to plot a synoptic (weather) chart. We would learn more about the latter when we arrived on a station, but for the present we had to commit to memory the Beaufort scale of wind strength; the many points of a compass; the realisation that one did not talk of 'rain' but of 'precipitation' (which means everything from drizzle to snow); the difference between mist and haze, and when mist becomes fog; and – most difficult of all – to differentiate between the many types of cloud, their height and their significance.

Many unprofitable hours were spent on the flat roof of the ex-department store, squinting hopefully into theodolites to spot weather balloons and track their course. These pilot balloons were made of rubber, filled with hydrogen from a cylinder and, supporting a standard weight, would rise through the air at 500ft a minute. The idea was to take a reading each minute through the theodolite and by means of some simple arithmetic it was possible, if you were clever enough, to calculate the wind strength as it varied from minute to minute at the different altitudes. I was obviously not clever enough, because all I succeeded in doing was to identify, at a distance of about two miles, the face of Big Ben – upside down. Occasionally a balloon would whizz across the view-finder, but as far as I was concerned this was purely accidental. Some of the other girls managed to get the hang of the theodolite pretty quickly, but I never did.

Somewhat easier to operate was the weather balloon which was released on cloudy days to determine the height of the bottom layer of cloud. While it rose at the usual 500ft per minute, all one had to do was stand by with a stop watch and note the exact second the balloon disappeared into cloud.

Some days it was difficult to concentrate when the weather was clear and sunny, and the view across London beneath the barrage balloons was inclined to draw all our eyes. London was recovering from the worst days of the blitz, and while there was an air raid from time to time, I don't recall that we ever had to leave our ninth floor bedrooms at night to flock down to the air raid shelters. More raids were to come later, but during our two months in the city it was all fairly peaceful. There were quite a lot of nasty gaps in the skyline from previous raids and I spent a lot of time while waiting for my turn at the theodolite, picking out landmarks and spotting bomb damage, when I should really have been observing the sky and trying to identify the clouds from the illustrations in my textbook. This is the kind of thing you can only learn by slow degrees, but once learnt you never forget and even now, forty odd years on, I only have to look once at a cloud for my mind to immediately register its type, height and meaning. It has become second nature for me to look at the sky and make my own mental weather forecast, and then congratulate myself if it concurs with the BBC's. Sometimes, of course, it doesn't and there have been occasions when I've been right and they have been very wrong, but that's another story.

We were introduced to the Stevenson Screen, without which no weather station can operate, and were assured that wherever we were sent we would find one of these. It was a white-painted box on legs, a bit like an elevated rabbit hutch with louvred sides, which housed a variety of thermometers, each of which would have to be read every hour and the readings noted down. There were maximum and minimum thermometers which recorded (not unnaturally) the max. and min. temperatures over a given period, and also a wet bulb and a dry bulb thermometer. The dry bulb thermometer gave the actual air temperature as it fluctuated during the day and night hours; the wet bulb thermometer had a damp muslin cloth around its mercury-filled bulb, which had to be kept wet with distilled water, and from the resulting drop in temperature due to evaporation it was possible to compute a mysterious thing called the 'dew point'. This is the temperature at which condensation sets in and the atmosphere is saturated. When aircraft are flying it is vitally important to know what the dew point is, because when the air is at saturation point all sorts of things which are death and destruction to aircraft can occur, like fog or icing on the wings.

Then there were other instruments to get to know – barometers and baragraphs, thermographs and hygrometers, wind anenometers on the roof, and rain guages and sunshine recorders. Also we had to discover how to judge distances in order to estimate the visibility, another vital factor when aircraft were taking off and landing. There did seem to be an awful lot to learn.

One of our RAF Instructors was heard to remark to a colleague that he considered it a waste of time to try teaching meteorology to Waafs as they were all as dim as Toc H lamps[1]. Of course, he wouldn't have got away with a chauvinistic comment like that in the 1980's, but this was 1943 and Women's Lib was not yet born, so we had to put up with his poor opinion of us.

I was one of the few who could go home at weekends, most of the others living much further away, and so were unable to bolster up their spirits with a bit of home cooking, comfortable beds, cups of tea brought up in the morning, etc. In any case, we all had friends and relations in one or other of the fighting zones, and sometimes our minds were not entirely on the job in hand.

It goes without saying that I lost no time in going home on my first weekend to show off my new uniform. I was the only girl in my family to get into uniform during the war. My cousin Louisa was simply livid with jealousy, as she had been trying to join the Waaf since the war started but was unable to obtain her release from her

[1] Toc H. An organisation started in Belgium during the First World War, as a hostel for the troops. It was run from Talbot House (its initials known in the language of the Morse Code as Toc H) in Poperinghe by a clergyman called Philip Byard Clayon, more familiarly known to his generation as 'Tubby'.

Toc H hostels subsequently spread throughout the world, but, like a lot of charitable organisations, they were always short of money, and the story is that the oil lamps hung outside the entrance to the hostels were always dim because of lack of oil, hence, 'dim as Toc H lamps'.

Civil Service job. So, to rub her nose in it, I suggested we both paid a visit to the local dance hall on my first Saturday in London, and we duly went – me, of course, wearing my uniform and she in her one good dress. It seems ridiculous, when I think of those thick grey lisle stockings and solid black shoes I was wearing, that I didn't sit out a single dance in the entire evening. Girls in uniform were still a bit of a novelty in Southgate. But the evening was made for me by one incident which I couldn't possibly have anticipated.

I was dancing a foxtrot with a tall, skinny youth who seemed to have two left feet (so I was thankful for once for the solidity of those aforementioned Waaf shoes), when a party of men in RAF uniform entered the hall. I gave them a casual glance, noting that they were obviously a few beers ahead of the rest of us and, as only soft drinks were obtainable in this particular hall, apparently now on the look-out for some female company. A night out for the boys, in fact. The face of one of them seemed familiar, so I looked again while my mind skipped back a few years – six, to be precise – when I was fifteen. My father had brought home from his London office a tall, young man who was new to the firm and was rather under Dad's wing. He was extremely good-looking, with regular features and black hair Bryl-creemed flat to his head, which was the fashion then. He came to our house several times for supper, and to my young impressionable mind he was a cross between Robert Taylor and Tyrone Power. Naturally, he didn't take much notice of me – I was still at school and he was at least twenty six then – but over the years I kept tabs on him, so to speak, and I knew that he had married and lived not far from us at Mill Hill. And now, unless I was very much mistaken, here he was before me in the flesh.

But could it *really* be him? He seemed to have shrunk a great deal and was even a bit round shouldered – not nearly as glamorous as I had pictured him all those years ago. There was only one way to find out. The next dance was a Ladies Excuse-me Waltz, so I waited until he was safely on the floor dancing with a large girl in a red dress, then I tapped him on the shoulder and took her place. I could tell at once that I was not what he had in mind for the rest of *his* evening – he'd seen plenty of Waafs on the airfield where he was stationed and now he was anticipating something a bit more fancy. We chatted a bit about this and that, and then I looked him straight in the eye and said, 'You don't remember me, do you?'

A glazed look came over his eyes and he shook his head. No, he didn't remember me. I thought I had better make sure of my facts. 'You are Ted Lord, aren't you? I'm Mr Huckle's daughter!'

The glazed look was replaced by one of sheer horror. You could almost see the thoughts whirling round in his brain – good heavens, here's someone who knows me, I'm supposed to be miles away back at base, what if this gets back to the wife? and so on. Luckily for his blood pressure, someone else soon claimed him for a dance, and the next time I looked around for him, he was gone – probably to find a telephone to reassure his wife that he was behaving himself, reading a good book in bed and wishing she was there.

Naturally, I *did* tell my father all about it, and he nearly fell off his chair, laughing. 'Old Teddy Lord!' he chortled. 'Caught out at last!' It was that month's best joke. I made him promise me that he wouldn't spread it around the office, but I could see that it was going to be hard to keep it to himself. Ted's wife, apparently, was the suspicious kind, and perhaps she had reason to be. But for me an illusion was shattered that evening. My handsome hero was in fact only an ordinary man, no better or worse than anyone else – and not even very good-looking now. I felt that I had suddenly grown up.

One Saturday morning, I paid a visit to my own office, the one I had been called up from, now evacuated to a requisitioned private house at Hadley Wood in Hertfordshire. Quite a lot of the men I had worked with were now missing from their desks, having been called up themselves over the past few months. We had worked together through the quiet months of the 'phony war', and then the whole office was sent out to this detached house in its own grounds, just in time for the Battle of Britain and the threatened invasion by the Germans. Although the majority of the air battles took place over southern and eastern England, there was still quite a lot going on from time to time in our area and air raid warnings, accompanied by the crump of bombs, were a frequent occurrence.

I remember one exciting afternoon in June 1940, when an air battle occurred right over our heads, between several German Dorniers and a whole array of Hurricanes swooping and diving around them. The bombers were on their way to attack some target near the Midlands – a ball-bearing factory at Luton it was whispered – and we heard the bombs landing, then the whole fleet came back again, once more chased by the fighters, and we had the satisfaction of seeing one of the bombers come down in flames. We were all out in the garden by then, running up and down cheering our boys on. It was all quite crazy and I'm afraid not much work was done for the rest of that day. It never entered our heads that the crashing bomber might have come down on some houses or a factory, or perhaps even a school.

On my visit, I was less than delighted to see that one of the staff who had not been a great favourite of mine, was still there at the same desk, dispensing his usual mixture of mealy-mouthed platitudes and downright despondency. He was an older man who had been in the First World

War – I've forgotten his name but it was something quite unremarkable – and according to his account, had spent the entire four years in the trenches eating bully beef sandwiches and drinking stewed tea. He was a Bore, with a capital B – but he was worse than that. As the summery days of 1940 passed, we woke up each morning expecting to see the clear blue skies filled with descending parachutists, but day followed day and nothing happened, except that we sensed from the brief BBC news bulletins that the Spitfire and Hurricane squadrons were fighting for their lives – and ours – and were gradually losing ground. Then it was that Mr X started getting on everyone's nerves by remarking that it was a pity we were fighting the Hun, they were good blokes the Jerries, he'd seen them in the First World War, good fighters they were, the Boche, they should be our Allies – it was them bloody Frenchies we should be fighting etc.

Well, I don't know what we could have done if the Germans had landed – not much, as we had nothing to fight them with except broom handles and pitchforks – but I do know who would have been in the front line, welcoming them to England, bowing to the ground and licking their boots. I could just see it. I suppose we should have reported him to someone – but who? – it hardly seemed worthwhile. He was really beneath our contempt and anyway he didn't do much harm, except perhaps to himself. He lost all his friends and his wife left him, so he ended the war a lonely and embittered man.

There were several married women now on the staff, something which would have been unheard-of before the war, and soon after my arrival on this visit, one of them, a Mrs Anne Withers, buttonholed me and gave me the story of her exciting experiences the previous weekend. Her husband was in the RAF, she informed me, stationed in a West Country seaside town for his Initial Training for Air Crew, and she was in the habit of travelling down there each weekend to be with him. On the last occasion, as she was on her way to the railway station early on the Monday morning to return home, there was a hit-and-run raid by a solitary enemy aircraft – which must have been the only time this particular town was attacked throughout the war – and, she announced, with her face blazing with righteous indignation, 'I was bombed and machine-gunned all the way up the road!', as if the bombs and machine-gun bullets had been aimed directly at her. My ever-active sense of the ridiculous nearly caused me to burst out laughing, but I did manage to restrain myself, merely asking if anyone had been hurt, but no, there hadn't even been any damage. However, I was evidently a disappointment to her and hadn't responded with the right amount of shock and amazement. I'm afraid I was beginning to feel a bit superior to mere civilians, quite wrongly of course, as I am sure in lots of ways civilians had the worst of the war, carrying on in their usual, humdrum jobs, being bombed and having to cope with food and clothing shortages, without the satisfaction of leaving home and being able to really do something active.

Back in London on the Met Course, I was still being dogged by J R Evans, who continued to be a thorn in my side by wanting to work with me in tandem, and as I was solitary by nature I had to carefully tell her that I preferred to work alone. 'Oh, you are a funny girl!' she once complained petulantly in the middle of a lesson, causing every eye to swing round and focus on me to see what extraordinary deed I had committed in broad daylight. Once again I wished for the floor to open up and swallow me.

In our off-duty time there was plenty of entertainment even in blacked-out London for those who didn't have nearby relatives to visit, and I know some girls were out every evening hitting the night spots. Presumably they had escorts with large bank accounts. My time in London coincided with the leave of a young Naval Officer with whom I had been to school in kindergarten days, and we saw quite a lot of each other during the evenings. He had been on a Royal Navy cruiser which was sunk by the Japanese in the Indian Ocean just prior to the fall of Singapore and had spent 30 hours in the water, first clinging to a raft and then in a small boat, watching the sharks circling round them. The smell of blood attracted them and the wounded were picked off, one by one, without anyone else being able to do anything about it. He only told me the bare details and once said he couldn't believe how lucky he was to be alive. He seemed to be happy to hang around in my company, going to dances and the cinema, but I think he was in a state of delayed shock most of the time and I don't suppose I was much help to him, except perhaps to make him laugh every now and again. I believe he was interested in carrying the friendship a bit further, but it wasn't the right time and he wasn't the right person. We parted good friends when I left London and he went to another ship, and was actually in the van at the invasion in 1944. I never saw him again.

When I was halfway through the course influenza swept through our ranks and I was one who succumbed to the infection, in spite of having felt so fit only a few weeks before. It was the worst dose of 'flu I had ever had, and when my temperature went up to 105° I think I had them worried in Sick Bay.

A Waaf doctor with a grim poker face and a clinical thermometer in her hand, strode into the ward that evening at 9pm to check this out, and by the way she felt all my joints and questioned me, I rather think she suspected rheumatic fever. Nothing was said to me, no word of explanation or even a smile to cheer me up a little, but I was put onto one of the earliest antibiotics called, I think, M & B 693. This rapidly brought my temperature down, at the same time making me feel so nauseous that I thought I would just as soon be dead anyway. Within five days I was said to be 'normal' and sent off home on forty-eight hours sick leave, barely able to stagger down to the bus stop.

Home was not very cheerful at that time. My young brother Ken was about to join the RAF and no further word had been heard about Cedric. At present he was still only missing, and when I arrived back on the course the following Monday, I made up my mind to see if I couldn't find out something of what had happened to him. After all, I was in the Air Force as well, wasn't I? It should be possible to dredge some information up from somewhere. So, in my ignorance of the correct procedure, I wrote a letter to the senior Waaf Officer at the block of flats where we lived, giving all the detalis, date he was shot down, etc, and asking for help in tracing his whereabouts. I posted the letter in the post box provided for our use in the downstairs entrance lobby, and waited for an answer. A few days later I was summoned to the presence of this same officer, who demanded to know why I had had the temerity to do such a thing. Apparently I had broken every rule in the book by going straight to the top. I should first have gone to my corporal, who would have passed the request on to her sergeant, and she in turn would have sent it on to the next in line, and so on, until either it got shot down in flames on the way or it finally reached someone with the authority to deal with it. It must have been patently obvious to everyone present that I was totally unaware of this procedure, and they very gently put me back on the tracks by telling me it was not possible to find anything out this way. The only thing to do was to contact the Red Cross and they would be the first to know if there were any further news.

This I did, and after a few weeks was informed that he was now officially missing, believed killed.

That was the point when all hope of Cedric's return died, at least for me. His parents went on hoping for a long time – he was their only child – but nothing further was ever heard. I believe his name is on the RAF memorial at Runnymede, the memorial to all those airmen who have no known grave, but I have never been to see it and I never shall. To me, to see the actual certainty of his death printed on a wall would destroy the memories of the living person. He was the most vividly alive person I have ever met and that is how I shall remember him.

As I had now missed a week of the course through being ill, I had to be put back to the next class, so all my former acquaintances were ahead of me. One consolation was that I no longer had J R Evans haunting me every day.

Instead, I made friends with a jolly little Scots girl named Sheila, who initiated me into the intricacies of Scottish dancing. She had many Scottish friends in London and they ran their own club for the dancing of reels and eating of haggis and general merry-making. I didn't know a Scottish reel from a cotton one but I was very soon won over, and if you haven't danced an eightsome reel to the bagpipes with several brawny Scots lads in kilts, then believe me, you haven't lived! For a shortie like me, it was the nearest thing to flying one could imagine, barring actually getting into an aeroplane. I began to wish I could boast of some Scottish blood myself. For sheer breathless, exhausting fun, an eightsome reel takes some beating.

And so I came up to the exams at the end of the two month course. They were not really too difficult, merely a general test to make sure we hadn't been wasting everyone's time. If one had managed not to get thrown off the course then all was well. One day we assembled to hear our postings read out, having previously been told that if we found we were not happy with our individual destinations and could find someone to change with, this would not be frowned upon. True to human nature, nearly everyone wanted to change and there was chaos and pandemonium for about half an hour. I was quite happy. My posting was to somewhere in Oxfordshire, not too far from the focus of all interest (ie, London), but a girl called Marigold came feverishly up to me and said her fiancé was stationed at the place I was going to, and would I *please* change or she would simply *die*. Well, it was all one to me really. I had no fiancé so I agreed and ended up instead at a small satellite station near Cambridge, which was probably more interesting anyway, as I found out later. At least it was a bomber station, whereas the place in Oxfordshire was for training aircrews only, but neither of us knew this at the time. I found I was able to get into Cambridge very easily, rapidly discovered what a beautiful town it was and spent a lot of my off-duty time there.

But that was later. First I had to get to my destination, with my kitbag full of my uniform and personal belongings. During this journey I was completely on my own, whereas before there had always been lots of us to help each other along. The way to carry a loaded kitbag is to swing it up onto your shoulder, but if you are only 5ft, 2ins tall and not too muscular, this is not the easiest thing in the world to do. With a tremendous effort I could swing it up to approximately shoulder level, but there was a fifty percent chance that I would miss my shoulder altogether and the wretched thing would thump down onto the ground on the other side, nearly up-ending me. If one could get it onto some fairly high object, like a shelf or a mantel-piece, then it was possible to ease it gradually into position, and after carefully getting the right balance, to stagger away slightly lop-sided and bow-legged. However, mantel-pieces are not too plentiful at railway stations and bus stops, which were the usual places I found myself struggling round, so the whole operation was difficult in the extreme. I usually ended up dragging it along behind me and trying to ignore the horrible rasping noise it made.

On this occasion, when I finally arrived at Cambridge railway station, an RAF corporal observed me trying to manhandle this awkward, heavy object and took pity on me. With great ease he heaved the loaded kitbag into the back of the waiting truck and then gave me a leg-up, straight into the laps of several RAF other ranks who were already seated inside, and who welcomed me with great conviviality – and then proceeded to enlighten me on the awfulness of the dump we were all bound for.

3

A new life begins

I must admit that, viewed in the near-dark of a wet April evening, Bourn was *not* a pretty sight.

The war had necessitated the hasty building of many temporary airfields all over the eastern side of England to house the aircraft and personnel required for the continuous night bombing of targets in Germany, and Bourn was one of them. At first sight the place seemed to consist of a huddle of rounded Nissen huts with cinder paths leading here and there, all looking dismal under the weeping, grey canopy of the sky. There were puddles everywhere, and a few grey-blue figures squelching from one hut to another. At the end of the main track was a more permanent looking two-storeyed building. This turned out to be the Control Tower, the nerve centre of the whole place, with the Flying Control office taking up the entire upper floor, while on the ground floor were the Meteorological Office, the Signals Office, the Telephone Exchange, and a mysterious place called Intelligence which lesser mortals such as I were not allowed to enter. On the far side of the Control Tower was a large empty space which I took, correctly, to be the airfield, and even as I watched an aircraft lumbered past, probably on its way round to the runway for take-off. I recognised the distinctive shape of a Stirling, having had a young brother in the Air Training Corps who had pictures on his bedroom walls of practically every aircraft ever built. This was proof, anyway, that I had finally arrived at the place where I most wanted to be. Cedric had flown Stirlings.

When I found myself and my kitbag deposited outside the Guard Room, my immediate concern after booking in was to present myself at the Met Office and announce, 'Hello, I'm the new Met Waaf,' or words to that effect. At this time, when so many girls were being admitted to the Forces and rapidly trained for the many different trades, this must have been a frequent occurrence up and down the country on Bomber, Fighter and Training RAF Stations. When I appeared at the door, I was greeted with equanimity and indeed made to feel welcome by the other two Waafs on duty and the Met Officer who was present, but I couldn't help feeling that they must have viewed me with sinking hearts and the identical thought, 'Oh God, not another one!' Especially as no-one had seen fit to inform them that I was on my way. I was well aware that two months' intensive training could not possibly have made any of us competent meteorological assistants, and we were all sent on our first postings to learn our trade. This meant that every Met observation we made had to be done with another experienced assistant, who patiently saw us through our first hopeless flounderings and ghastly mistakes. At first I was hopeless. We were *all* hopeless.

The office itself was pleasantly light and airy, with windows on two sides giving unrestricted views across the airfield. On the other side of the main cinder road was another building which was the Navigation Office and the air crews' Briefing Room. This is where the crews received their instructions on flying days before taking off on bombing raids, and where they had to report back on their return. They very often came across to the Met Office after de-briefing to tell us how right (or wrong) our weather forecast had been. We got to know all of them by sight, a lot by name, some for only a short spell of time and others, the survivors, for longer.

On this, the day of my arrival, after I had introduced myself and been handed a cup of coffee, I stood by the fire looking round and taking stock. There was a long plotting bench down the centre of the room, where a fair-haired Waaf was feverishly scratching away on a chart from a long scroll of white paper, and the Met Officer was explaining the synoptic situation to several Air Crew Officers and Sergeants. Everyone seemed to be extremely busy, with no time to spare for a new, very junior ACW2. I gathered that it was going to be an operational night. After a few moments, the two most senior officers swept out, and by the way everyone flattened themselves against the wall as they passed, and the sighs of relief which followed their departure, it was pretty obvious even to a rookie like me that they were very senior indeed and also not too pleased with the weather prospects for the night. I didn't know until some time later that I had arrived in the middle of Bomber Command's first great offensive against the Ruhr, which had started the previous month, and from the moment I started work (the next day), I was totally immersed in the day by day and night by night drama of what was taking place.

But that first day I had no part in it. I knew my place in the general order of things was right down at the bottom of the heap and in any case, first thing first, I had to get down to the Waaf site, book in there, find my bed and unpack. I was taken in a truck down the long road to the site which was a mile away from the operational centre, and driven by a chatty LAC who commiserated with me all the way on my misfortune at being posted to this 'dead, dirty dump' – as he called it. Somewhat depressed, I listened in silence as he pointed out to me on the left hand side the Administrative buildings and the Sergeants' and Airmens' Messes, and then at the bottom of the hill we turned right, down yet another cinder road, to the ten Nissen huts which comprised the Waaf living quarters. It was dark by this time so I couldn't see much, and as I groped my way to the door of the Waaf Guard Room, my companion drove off, with one last cheerful thought which he directed to me from the truck window, 'You know, you're all only one field away from the end of the main runway!'

Nevertheless, my reception in the Waaf Guard Room was cheerful enough. The corporal on duty *did* know I was coming, was pleased to hear that I was a Met Office Waaf as she knew they were very short-staffed up there, and she then directed another Waaf to take me to Hut 4. In the all-enveloping darkness, I had no idea what the general area looked like, but the blaze of light and chatter of female voices which greeted me as I stepped inside the hut was reassuring. 'Another new one,' said the Waaf, and melted away into the dark.

It was a long room I stepped into with about twenty beds altogether, arranged against the walls on either side, each bed with a locker and shelves over the top for books or photographs. At the end, next to the door, was one bed in an alcove with slightly more space than the others, and this was allocated to the corporal in charge of the hut. The area around each bed was known as its bed-space and this had to be kept clean and tidy, with clothes put away in the locker and a minimum of books and personal items left around. Instead of mattresses there were 'biscuits' – large, square, fairly solid cushions which when put end to end made a mattress, three to a bed, and which had to be stacked one on top of the other each morning at the head of the bed. In the middle of the hut was the inevitable cast-iron coke stove, from which came a welcome heat, and girls in various stages of undress were sitting around it, drinking cocoa, knitting or writing letters.

They were all very cordial. I was glad of this because by now I was feeling rather low, what with wet feet and having had no solid food for several hours, and above all, being cast pell-mell into yet another strange place with a whole lot of new faces to get used to. Most of the girls, they told me, worked on shift at the operational end of the camp, in the Met Office or Signals or Flying Control and they all sympathised with me that I had been unfortunate enough to end up here, as apparently Bourn was a very new station and a bit short on amenities. I was beginning to get a bit tired of people telling me how unlucky I was to be there. My main feeling was relief that I could at last sit down and change my shoes, and to know that this iron bedstead I was sitting on actually had my name over the top and was my place to relax. I had been issued with two towels in the Waaf Guard Room, or Picquet Post as it was called, and now I was informed that the bath water was hot and I could go across to the bath huts and have a soak any time I liked. Apparently the hot water system had been out of action for a week owing to some breakdown in the plumbing, but it had that day been restored. Janet, the Signals girl, said that she had just taken her first hot bath for a week and had been lying in steaming water for the past half hour, watching the scum rise to the top. Well, I hadn't been expecting luxuries, and at least there was electricity and flush loos, so sitting round the stove eating someone' home baked cakes and drinking someone else's cocoa, I was happy and felt I had at last arrived somewhere. As it turned out, this place would be my home for the next two years.

The two Met girls who were present were to be my companions for the next two years. Mary and Freda had only been at Bourn for two and four weeks respectively, straight from Met school in London the same as me, and what we knew about practical meteorology could have fitted on a postage stamp. We therefore helped each other when on duty, doing every task in pairs, being wrong most of the time but being ably helped by Sandy, the girl I had already met up in the office, and Corporal Jane, she with her bed in the corner of the hut. All that could be seen of Jane at the moment was a mound of grey blankets, as she was trying to get some sleep prior to going on night duty. She and Sandy had been Met Waafs for over a year and were alarmingly competent.

It was all rather like being a new girl at school, 'What's your name? How old are you? Where do you live?' Only here it was more likely to take the form of, 'What's your name? Where do you live?' and, 'Do you have a boyfriend?' If the answer to the last question was 'yes' – 'Is he in the RAF?' Mary's was a Flight Sergeant stationed in the north of England; Freda's was in the Navy, and I didn't have one. Most of the girls referred to the man in their life as 'My Man', and if you didn't have a man then you were regarded as rather a poor fish. I got the message pretty quickly so I resurrected poor Cedric and then became the centre of much interest and sympathy. I was advised not to give up hope, lots of men became prisoners of war, no news was good news, etc. Feeling a bit uncomfortable I tried to change the subject by enquiring what time supper was, and this produced an immediate bustle of activity with much cleaning of shoes, changing of shirts and quick dashes out to the ablutions.

Two of the Signals girls, Billie and Frankie, were also getting ready to go to the Mess, with Gladys and Megan (telephonists). I wondered then, and I still wonder, at the number of girls who affected boys' names – although I did eventually find out that Billie's real name was Agnes. But there were Johnnies and Jackies and Bobbies, and they were all popular, good-looking girls who seemed to have dates most nights. If you wanted to be a social success, you got yourself a boy's name! Megan was a happy little Welsh girl with a non-stop voice, and Gladys a plump, bottle blonde who had an American sergeant in the background and affected a pseudo American accent.

After a while we all trooped out to the Airmen's Mess for supper, which again was not the Ritz but the food was hot and there was plenty of it. The Mess was a large hangar-like building with a counter at one end where the cooks were dishing out the food, and long trestle tables across the width of the room with benches to sit on. The Waafs occupied one table at the far end. With mug, and knife, fork and spoon ('irons') in our hands we joined the queue which stretched right round to the door. I was struck by the staggering number of airmen compared with the very few Waafs – lines of them in Air Force blue; tall, short, fat, thin, queueing up like us with their mugs and irons, forage caps either balanced on their right ear or stuffed through the epaulets of their battle dress. Nobody took any notice of me – I was just one more new face amongst hundreds of others coming or going all the time. It would seem perhaps that this was a paradise for an unattached female, with all these men around, but it didn't work out like that. It's true a few romances did blossom, but most people at that time in the Air Force were working far too hard and for such long hours that there were not all that number of permanent relationships resulting. A lot of men still didn't like to see women in uniform, which was hard luck on those of us who had to wear it.

The NCOs from sergeants upwards, and the officers, had their own separate messes and we didn't meet up with them except in the course of our work.

I was told that we had to be back in the Waaf site by 10.30pm unless we obtained a late pass, in which case we were to be Cinderellas and get back by midnight. Breakfast was at 8am and morning parade at 8.45am. One good thing about being a shift worker was that it was nearly always possible to avoid morning parade altogether. We were either working on the day shift which started at 8am, or sleeping after night duty, which ended at 8am, or standing in for someone else. One way or another we usually managed to dodge it.

The Waafery was under the care and administration of a Waaf Officer, General Duties, one Section Officer O'Malley – or Miss Malley as we called her. Everything in our daily lives which went wrong was blamed on Miss Malley. If late passes were cancelled it was her fault, if the mail didn't yield up the one letter you were waiting for, she must have dropped it down the back of her desk, and so on. Every now and then we had a kit inspection and that really did bring out the worst in her. All our kit had to be laid out on our beds in rigid order – shirts, skirts, undies, shoe brushes, brass polish, everything, with shoes in line at the end all the way down the hut. Then round would come Miss Malley, red-faced, officious and eagle-eyed, and if the smallest item was missing we either had to account for it or pay up. Dirty shoes always called for a few terse comments. Those of us who were not neat and tidy by nature when we entered the Waaf soon became so of necessity. Rather more rarely we had inspections by the Commanding Officer of the whole station, and for this major event everything had to *shine*, including those Waafs who were unfortunate enough to be off-duty at the time and were therefore present, standing by their beds, when the great man came round. When one of these inspections was due, Miss Malley was crabby and distracted for days beforehand and we all kept out of her way as much as possible.

She was the perpetual target for moans and complaints, but she really wasn't a bad old stick – and not so old either, except to our youthful, prejudiced eyes. She was always on hand if anyone was in trouble, ready to grant 48-hour leaves if your boyfriend was home or your parents ill. Her one obsession was neatness. She liked to see the hut with beds geometrically at right-angles to the walls, the biscuits neatly stacked, personal gear as much out of sight as possible, and her eternal grouse at us shift girls was that we didn't sleep *tidily*. She really didn't like to see anyone sleeping in the daytime – it upset the general symmetry of the hut. Once she came bouncing in on an inspection early in the morning, when I had just climbed into my pyjamas and was on the verge of floating off into blissful sleep after a very hectic night duty. Gladys, who had also been up all night manning the switchboard next to the Met Office, hadn't even bothered to undress and lay flat out on the top of her bed, fully clothed and snoring. Miss Malley, charging down the length of the hut at her usual high speed, was pulled up short by this unedifying sight. 'And who's this,' she snorted, indignantly, 'in a huddle of dirty shoes on the bed?' There was a small silence, and then Megan, hoping to smooth ruffled feathers, replied silkily that it was LACW Smith, Ma'am, who had been working all night, and added, a trifle unwisely, 'Well, she has put her curlers in, Ma'am.' This remark was not well received. Miss Malley knew perfectly well, as we all did, that Gladys had probably had them in all night, trading on the fact that, tucked away in her little cubby hole with the switchboard she was not on general view and could get away with small deviations from the accepted rules of behaviour, whereas those of us who might come face to face with a Group Captain or a Wing Commander at any time during an operational night, had to at least keep our hair combed and our jackets buttoned up. Poor Miss

Malley, she had an unenviable job really, looking after the welfare of two hundred girls from all walks of life, away from home restrictions probably for the very first time, and she certainly didn't get any thanks for it. Later on, a special empty hut was allocated for the use of those of us who had to sleep in the daytime, so that we could sleep as untidily as we liked and wouldn't be disturbed by day workers coming in and out at lunchtime. Naturally, we all objected to this most strongly at first, but before long found that we could sleep there much more peacefully.

On my first day, by the time we arrived back at the Waaf Site from the Mess, the air was full of the roar of heavy aircraft taking off. As we were situated so near to the end of the main runway, when the wind was in the west the noise of the aircraft lumbering over our heads was hair-raising, until you got used to it. They were all heavily laden with high explosive and incendiary bombs and sounded as if they had great difficulty in getting off the ground at all. I dared not wonder what would happen to us if one didn't manage to lift off, or crashed when only a few feet up. I was to hear horrifying stories of just such an accident which happened on a nearby aerodrome, when a loaded bomber crashed on take-off and the Waafs had to be rushed out of bed to form a human chain with buckets of water to put out the fire. But while I was at Bourn we were lucky and this did not occur.

At first I didn't think I would ever get used to this nightly lullaby, but it is amazing how repetition dulls apprehension and after a short time I was able to sleep through most take-offs and landings. It was a bit like the 1940 blitz on London, when we finally managed to sleep through the heaviest of anti-aircraft gunfire; in fact through anything except a really *close* near-miss. That is, we young ones did. I believe, on reflection, that the whole filthy uproar must have been rather harder on the nerves of the middle-aged and elderly. Only as I've grown older myself have I begun to appreciate just what effect the bombing had on my parents' generation. They had after all been through what was thought to be the 'war to end all wars' only twenty years previously, and here it was happening all over again, only worse.

On this night, I lay rigid in my bed as aircraft after aircraft throbbed into the air, and I know that Mary, who had a nervous disposition, was also lying awake in the next bed. Finally, she whispered to me, 'Nineteen, that's the lot.' Then we could only hear the distant noise of aircraft taking off from neighbouring airfields, until even that died away and the peace of the East Anglian countryside surrounded us.

The next day really was the start of a whole new life, although the first thing to happen was quite mundane. I had to go along to the Stores to collect my battledress. For everyday work and wear, those of us who worked part of the time in the open were issued with a blue serge blouse top and trousers, and our jackets and skirts were henceforth kept for parades and state occasions. The battledress was much more comfortable to wear and, best of all, had no brass buttons to be polished. I even managed to get one which fitted fairly well and only needed the trouser legs turning up – a simple task which was soon done.

The next problem was getting about the camp, where every building was about a mile from the next one. The obvious answer was a bicycle, and we were all issued with these as soon as we arrived. They were very basic vehicles, without any refinements such as gears, or even brakes in some cases, and any small additions we made, such as front and rear lamps, had to be guarded with our lives or nailed down, otherwise they had a strong tendency to disappear. I was allocated the most rickety and rusty of bikes, which had probably been rejected and handed down by a long line of Waafs before me, and I made a mental note to upgrade this at the first opportunity. I had not ridden a bike for several years but as with a lot of other skills, once you can do it you have it for life. After several wobbly practice runs round the Waaf site, I reckoned I was capable of venturing out in the direction of the Mess, and apart from one or two forced landings in the first few days, I managed fairly well.

Not like Polly, one of the typists in the Administration Centre, a large girl with no sense of balance, who had great difficulty in learning how to ride, and had to have a girl on either side of her for days while she struggled to master her bicycle, with many a shriek as she collapsed onto the ground. The day Polly finally managed a circuit of the Waaf cinder track was a red-letter day in her life, but like most people who take up bicycle riding as adults, she was never very good at it, any more than I was. I was never a terribly accomplished cyclist, being liable to fall off in nervous moments and not being very adept at mounting it without a convenient kerb at hand, but on most small satellite airfields the distances between the various buildings necessitated some form of transport apart from shanks's pony, so a bike it had to be.

One thing I always dreaded and tried to avoid was cycling up the hill to work while take-off was in progress, as the road crossed the end of the runway. Once, by mistake, I was actually cycling across as a loaded aircraft staggered over my head. I was totally deafened for a few minutes, and petrified out of my wits. After that I always waited at the edge until the coast was clear before venturing across. It was frightening even to stand at the edge of the runway and watch these great monsters hurtling towards you, and knowing what a disaster could occur if the pilot made the slightest error, or if any mechanical failure occurred at the vital moment of lift-off. Actually these things happened very rarely, such was the dedication to their work of air and ground crews alike. I had tremendous admiration for them, and still have.

One of the Met Officers had a BSA motorbike and would occasionally give us nerve-wracking lifts into Cambridge on his pillion seat, but for getting round the camp, if at any time our bicycles happened to be out of action, we had to hitch a lift on any four-wheeled vehicle which came into view. And with the chronic shortage of bicycle lamps, it was a common thing after dark to see convoys of cyclists shooting about the camp, the one in front having the lamp, the last one with the rear light, and those in the middle in stygian darkness. You had a good excuse if you saw someone you wanted to avoid, 'Sorry, couldn't stop – I was in convoy!'

One episode I remember which was rather funny, although I didn't see the funny side of it till later, happened when I was cycling up the hill to work one morning and decided to take a short cut via the perimeter track which went all round the edge of the airfield. This was strictly forbidden for reasons of safety, but I regret to say we all did it. I was pedalling along, my mind on other things, when I became aware that all was not as it should be. There was a strange noise behind me which was getting louder all the time, and when I looked round I realised I was being followed by a Stirling on its way round to its dispersal point. This enormous thing was towering above me, and of course the faster I pedalled, the faster it went. I could see five grinning faces looking down at me from the perspex cabin windows, and it must have been a great joke to them, one small Waaf pedalling frantically to get away from them. Eventually, I had the wit to pull off the track and let it go by me, and I arrived in the office feeling extremely foolish and hoping this episode had not been observed by my workmates, or I should never live it down. Actually I don't think anyone did notice it, for nothing was ever said to me about it.

I can never think of Waafs on bicycles without remembering Peggy, who worked in Flying Control. She was a country girl from Sussex who viewed life perpetually through rose coloured glasses and beamed at everyone indiscriminately. Peggy approaching on her bicycle was like a cheshire cat in reverse. First appeared the smile in the distance, followed by the rest of Peggy pedalling like mad. I don't think I ever saw her without the toothy smile – she even woke up smiling, especially if she had recently received a letter from her boyfriend in the army in the Middle East, the excruciating details of which she would insist on reading out loud in the hut to anyone who was within earshot. Sometimes she was hard to take, especially before breakfast.

I went up the hill for my first afternoon duty with Corporal Jane, of whom I was greatly in awe at this stage. She was tall, dark, thin as a whip and as smart as paint. She had a sharp wit and an even sharper tongue, but she was a good Met Assistant and helped me tremendously. After a week or two we became good friends and used to go into Cambridge regularly to browse in the bookshops and drink endless cups of coffee essence. It was pouring with rain and the wind was blowing strongly from the west as we set out, wearing our rain capes, a most unflattering garment which seemed to be designed more to let the rain run down our necks than to keep us dry. We must have resembled a couple of bell tents on wheels as we battled our way up the hill and the wind repeatedly got underneath our capes and threatened us with lift-off all the way up to the office. Jane's language was colourful to say the least, and I grinned to myself, thinking, yes I am going to like you, even if you are my senior.

The camp seemed almost deserted. No-one was out of doors who didn't have to be, and the aircraft could be seen standing at the various dispersal points, like grey, grounded beasts. One thing was certain – with the cloud almost on the ground and visibility no more than a hundred yards, there would be no flying that day, so it was a good chance to get the hang of the routine work of the office without any distractions.

4

'Was it a red sky this morning?'

One of the first things to happen after my arrival at Bourn was the phasing out of Stirling bombers, so that the one that followed me around the perimeter track must have been one of the last to operate from there. They were all replaced with Lancasters, which were to prove the backbone of the whole RAF heavy bomber force. At about the same time that this happened, Bourn became part of 8 Group, the Pathfinder Group.

Bomber Command was divided into Groups, each of which consisted of a Headquarters and up to a dozen satellite airfields scattered around it in the countryside, from East Anglia up to Yorkshire. Bomber Command itself was situated at High Wycombe in Buckinghamshire and from there the orders were sent out every day to each Group Headquarters, indicating which target had been selected for that night's operation, and the Groups then sent on the information to the Commanding Officers at each of the airfields, or 'out-stations'. About the middle of 1942 it became evident that in order to make the night bombing raids over Germany more effective, some form of air marking would have to be developed to guide the aircraft more accurately to their targets. Very often heavy cloud over the target area would completely obscure it and the bombs were sometimes dropped more by luck than good judgement and often in quite the wrong places, with the resulting waste of time and armament and unnecessary loss of life. And so 8 Group came into being, with selected Pathfinder crews carrying special coloured flares, or Target Indicators, to drop over the target area and show the following main force bomber crews where to unload their bombs. They were mostly crews who had successfully completed one tour of operations (30 missions), so they were not only skilful but also lucky. As Pathfinders they had the extra advantage of being able to use all the latest radar equipment to enable them to see through the layers of cloud, and when they were talking to Met Officers we would hear mysterious references to 'Gee' and 'H2S'. It was all fascinating stuff and very secret. 8 Group was led by Group Captain Donald Bennett, who we heard was a most formidable gentleman from 'down under' and who was mostly to be found at Group Headquarters, Huntingdon or at Wyton RAF Station, a few miles away. One hopes that Wyton, being a pre-war station, had a few more amenities than Bourn, which apparently had only recently been carved out of the mud.

As far as I was concerned, when I had been at Bourn a month I felt I had lived there for years.

After the initial strangeness had worn off, routine took over and I started to get used to meteorological work and enjoy it. Our days and nights were ruled by the clock. Every hour the assistant on duty had to read the instruments, make a note of the wind speed and direction, the visibility, the cloud, precipitation (if any), and whether the barometer was rising or falling, and then stand by to teletype the details in code to Group

Headquarters, who in turn would transmit it to Bomber Command. Next to the Met Office was the teleprinter room where yards of paper would come spewing out from the machine at regular intervals, bearing coded weather reports from all the other Met Stations in the United Kingdom and a few weather ships in the Atlantic, and these had to be painstakingly plotted on blank charts of the British Isles. This teleprinter machine was a temperamental beast and had to be carefully watched to make sure it didn't run out of paper, or chew it into shreds or otherwise make a mess of things, and it was one of our duties as Met Assistants to keep it in order. I suppose it was the predecessor of the modern telex, but it was an unreliable piece of equipment and we never knew when it was going to misbehave and we might have to send for the mechanic to come and unclog its innards.

There were occasions, also, when the assistant on duty would forget the time, and suddenly realise it was two minutes to the hour and she'd forgotten to do the observation. Then followed a mad rush out to the instruments, a frantic look at the sky and the visibility, a quick scribbling on a pad to write out the message, and a scramble into the teleprinter room to tap it out. By this time the bell would be ringing insistently, because the Met Waaf at Group who was collecting the observations would have her finger on it, and sometimes she would type out a terse little message or two, such as, 'Wake up, Bourn!' or 'There's a war on, you know!' After a few months of this kind of thing, it was a wonder we didn't automatically walk out of our homes every hour, on the hour, when we were on leave, to look at the weather.

As Bourn was such a new station, we only had the bare essentials in the way of equipment, mainly the Stevenson Screen with its thermometers, an aneroid barometer in the office and the aforementioned teleprinter. Our screen was situated outside the office on a patch of grass, reached by the usual cinder path, and was right on the edge of the airfield. The wind speed and direction, and the cloud height and type were major hurdles to be overcome each hour. At least, this is how Mary, Freda and I felt for the first few weeks. It was all very well reading about the clouds in books and studying the illustrations, but when faced with a sky full of different shapes and colours, we were frequently baffled. The clouds could have been at any height from fifty feet to six miles. But it's amazing how quickly you pick it up, especially if you happen to be interested in the work.

Working out the visibility was easier as we did have guidelines here – a tree on the other side of the airfield was at 1,000 yards, a distant farmhouse 2 miles, and if you couldn't see the briefing room it was foggy. And in order to assess the wind speed, we had to climb up a perpendicular outside iron staircase, which took us onto the flat roof of Flying Control. As Bourn did not boast an anemometer we had to quickly learn wind speed by other means, such as how much or how little the trees were bending in the wind and whether the distant windsock was at full stretch or hanging limply from its staff. As we negotiated the slippery rungs of that staircase, there were always a few interested bystanders with nothing better to do than shout encouraging remarks from time to time, but we soon learnt to ignore them. To be a girl surrounded by all these men, it was sometimes wise to pretend to be deaf.

Every three hours the Met Assistant had to plot a chart – that is, working from the coded symbols sent on the teleprinter, draw up on a large blank map of Great Britain the weather at that time over the whole country. We worked with two pens in the one hand, one for black ink and one for red, and at each weather station we had to draw in the symbols for wind speed and direction, barometric pressure, temperature, cloud type, amount and height, and precipitation, all in black, and the wet bulb temperature and dew point in red. After a few months of doing this several times each day and night, most of us could plot at the same speed as the information came in on the teleprinter. When each chart was finished, the Met Officer on duty had to join up all the points of equal barometric pressure, rather like joining numbers in a child's drawing book, and a weather map would emerge. Any approaching troughs of wet weather were drawn in as lines, either a warm front or a cold front, and many isobars close together meant high winds. A lack of isobars however was not necessarily good as it could indicate an area of high pressure, and in winter this usually meant fog. And that, of course, meant grounded aircraft, or even worse, very difficult landings if they were already airborne.

To be a Met Assistant you didn't have to understand the reason why the weather did this or that, you only had to record what was happening and make sure the officer in charge knew what was going on. Ours not to reason why – ours just to read the ruddy instruments and let others sort the problems out. Met Assistants were not supposed to give weather forecasts. This was the prerogerative of the Met Officer and I for one was quite happy with this state of affairs. After we had been constantly studying the sky for a few months and getting the feel of things, we did tend to develop a sixth sense regarding the weather, a bit like farmers. We were of course much hampered by the lack of weather reports to the west of us, as most of our weather comes from the west and Eire, being neutral in the war, didn't supply us with any reports. Even today weather reports are sometimes incorrect owing to the vagaries of our climate, but then, with the whole of western Europe blanked out (thanks to Hitler), together with most of Ireland, we were very dependant on the few Atlantic weather ships and (eventually) our own trained eyes to tell us what was coming.

By the very nature of our work, we Met girls knew many more of the air crews than we did of the ground staff. With the briefing room so near to our office, the flying boys were in and out quite frequently, as I have mentioned. They liked to check on the weather situation after briefing – they knew very well their lives could depend on the forecast. Quite often operations could be cancelled at the last moment owing to worsening weather conditions, and this must have been a terrible let-down for them, after getting themselves keyed-up for yet another hectic night. Some of them were really interested in meteorology, others only tolerant of what they considered to be a very inexact science. We used to come in for a fair amount of ribbing and good-natured chaff, and remarks like, Was it a red sky this morning? How's the old seaweed? and Bet you haven't looked out of the window lately! It was very noticeable, the difference in their attitudes before and after operations. Beforehand they were tense and quiet, and no doubt very frightened if the truth were known, but on their return, if we saw them at all, they would be relaxed and only looking forward to bacon and eggs in the Mess – and then bed.

We used to work eight hour shifts – morning, evening and night – and of these the night duties were at the same time the most boring and the most exciting, depending on whether there was anything 'on'. The Met, Signals and Switchboard girls all worked on the same ground floor, next to each other, and at the end of the corridor were the girls in the Intelligence office, although they didn't mix with us so much. Nevertheless we were very glad to have someone to talk to in the long reaches of the night when we were struggling to keep our eyes open. Round about midnight our supper was delivered to us from the cookhouse in a thing called a 'haybox'. This was a large, round, pail-like utensil with an inner lining and straw packed tightly into the space between for insulation, and usually containing some sort of stew. It looked like something indescribable, but I must admit it smelt and tasted good, and anyway we were all starving and would have eaten a horse. I will refrain from the obvious comment, and merely state that Air Force food was usually good, if a bit basic, and we came off better in that department than civilians.

One of the Signals assistants was male, a Leading Aircraftsman whose name I cannot now recall, but I will call him Fred. He looked like a Fred to me, being short, shaggy, pimply and with a big nose, and we were all delighted when he was on night duty with us because he then got the job of hauling the heavy haybox into the building and ladling out large dollops of this unidentifiable meal onto our plates. He was a good soul, was Fred. He saved one of the Signals Waafs from getting into trouble through not turning up for duty on time, simply by staying at his post until she finally did appear. It was one of those nights when there was a great deal of weather outside, and the girl in question, we knew, had spent the evening in the village pub with a group of others, male and female, from the station. When she didn't appear, we thought she was having bicycle trouble and was having to walk. What actually happened was that she somehow became separated from the others, decided to walk to work and fell in a ditch on her way up the hill. At 2am this terrible object loomed in the doorway, soaking wet and stone-cold sober, with the beginnings of a beautiful black eye. Somehow we got her mopped up and dried off, changed into dry clothes and made to look presentable in case any nosey parker in authority happened to look in. Luckily the weather was so awful that nothing was flying, so there was only routine work to attend to. Poor girl, she was eternally grateful to Fred, especially as the next day, after she'd slept it all off, she couldn't remember any of the details of that night.

Night duty was always interesting if 'ops' were on. We could hear the aircraft revving up at their dispersal points and then one by one taking off, labouring to get their weight off the ground before they ran out of runway. Soon the fading sky would be full of bombers from neighbouring airfields and others further north, all on their way to the same distant target – Hamburg, Berlin, the Ruhr. It was an awe-inspiring sight to stand in the dusk outside the office, watching and listening to the boys going out on what we all knew would be a hazardous and dangerous mission, from which at least some of them would not return. When they had gone and the noise of the engines had faded away, all would be quiet for a few hours and most people on night duty could relax – but not the Met Office, of course. Every hour on the hour there we were, slaves to that teleprinter machine and its little bell. Going down the cinder path to the screen in the dark, with our one feeble torch, was always horrendous because of the rats scuttling across the path. Once a Met Officer remarked cheerfully to me (from the warmth and light of the office), that the rats were much more frightened of me than I was of them, but I noticed that he didn't take me up on my suggestion that he should come out with me and see for himself.

About three in the morning was the worst time of all, when we were at our lowest ebb. The heating in the Met Office was by means of an open coke fire, and this we kept stoked up high on cold nights, but I'm not sure that this was such a good idea. The fumes from the coke had the effect of making us dopy, so that it was even more difficult to keep our eyes open. The crews were given caffeine tablets to keep them awake during the long flights and sometimes we managed to get hold of a few. I *always* found the night duties a great strain, and often had to walk up and down outside to clear my head with some fresh air. Endless cups of coffee helped a bit but what a relief it was to see the first pale streaks of dawn creeping across the sky. I don't think I had ever watched the dawn break until my Waaf days – certainly I had never stayed up all night before, and however many times I had to do it in the course of my duties, it always seemed to me a highly unnatural procedure. Night is for sleeping, not working.

About half an hour before the return of the aircraft on operational nights we would wake up the duty Met Officer, who was usually snoozing in the ante-room, so that he could mug up on the weather situation before the first of the returning crews came in. One after another the aircraft came back and we would count them, hoping against hope that they would all return. Nearly always one at least was missing, and that meant that seven men we all knew had got the chop. We saw so many of these bomber boys pass before us – we got to know them slightly and then they were gone. None of them were ready to die, but all of them knew the odds stacked against them. The rear gunners seemed to be the most at risk. At that time the flying life of a rear gunner on heavies was about nine hours. I soon decided it was a mug's game to get emotionally involved with any aircrew, as they were killed off with such regularity.

I sat in the office one afternoon when I was off-duty, toying with the usual coffee and a wad (a hard NAAFI bun of indeterminate ingredients), watching a young aircrew Sergeant Wireless Op/Air Gunner whom I knew slightly. He had been going out intermittently with our Corporal Jane, who was beginning to get very excited about him, and I must admit he was very good-looking. He was also invariably courteous and soft-spoken. Not for him the slightly raucous ribaldry with which most of the chaps used to greet us, no slaps on the rear or tweaking of curls, or addressing us as 'darling' or 'my love'. He was a nice, quiet, well brought up lad who would have been welcomed by any girl's mother as prospective husband material. Today he was quiet all right, standing and looking at the weather maps with the rest of his crew, smoking a cigarette with jerky hands. He glanced up once but looked right through me, and there was panic and disaster in his eyes. I knew the squadron was ordered out that night and he would be amongst them, and if ever death was in the face of a man, it was in his that afternoon. He knew he was doomed and there was nothing he could do about it.

I never forgot his face, and sure enough a few nights later his aircraft was one of those that failed to return.

Few of the missing were ever seen again. Some of the lucky ones took to their parachutes and spent the rest of the war in Germany – perhaps 'lucky' is not the right word, but at least they were alive. A very few ditched in the Channel and were picked up by Air Sea Rescue, but the majority were posted 'missing, believed killed' and were never heard of again.

We had heard that there were escape routes through France and Spain, but naturally none of us knew any of the details. This was the way I always imagined Cedric would get home, if he ever did, but the only person I knew who did manage to negotiate the mysterious overland route was a Lancaster pilot on one of our neighbouring stations and he did the whole thing, from being shot down to arriving back in England, in three weeks. This was remarkably quick by any standards. He must have been a remarkable man, because when his aircraft was shot down he lost his right hand but before many months had passed he was back on his squadron with a hook on his right arm, and although I am not one hundred percent sure of my facts here, I believe he went back on operations as a navigator or air gunner.

One night I remember clearly was when we lost an aircraft and crew at Bourn, not over Germany but back on our own airfield, which made it worse. It was my rest day but I knew how many aircraft had taken off, and as the sky lightened with the early summer dawn, we waited tensely in Hut 4 for them to return. The wind was easterly so they would be returning over our heads onto the main runway, and as the aircraft started to come back they seemed to be only a few feet above us, touching down after they crossed the far hedge. We lay in bed and counted them, knowing that only eight had gone out. Seven came back quite close together, then there was a heart-stopping silence which went on and on. After what seemed like several hours but was probably only a few minutes, we heard an aircraft approaching, and heads popped up all over the hut. It came nearer and it didn't sound right. The usual heavy roar of four Merlin engines was muted – it sounded as if it was limping. Breathlessly we heard it trundle over our heads, knew it was almost home – then there was one little 'pop', and silence. Everyone rushed outside in pyjamas and bare feet and there across the field the aircraft lay, on fire from wingtip to wingtip, with the broken-off tail section a few feet away. Knowing that the crew must all have been in the centre of the fuselage at crash stations, we also knew they must all be dead. There was total quiet except for the crackle of flames. We stared in stunned shock, realising that the pilot must have made one last superhuman effort not to come down right on our heads, but then just couldn't manage those last few yards which would have brought them safely onto the runway. There was nothing to say and nothing we could do. It was a perfect summer dawn and the red flames matched the red disc of the sun as it rose over the misty hedges.

But life was not all drama and tragedy. There was also the lighter side to things, like the day a high-ranking

RAF officer paid us a visit from Group Headquarters, the reason for which escapes me now. When he took off on his return flight in a small twin-engined plane, one of the engines failed, and the pilot, whether by accident or design I don't know, did a swift turn and made an emergency landing back on the airfield, missing the Control Tower by about three feet. I was cycling up the hill at the time to go on duty, and I nearly fell off my bike in my certainty that there was going to be a nasty accident. However, the only disaster occurred inside the Tower, where the duty staff dived to the floor when it looked as if the port wing was going to come through the window and a bottle of red ink emptied itself down the right sleeve of Flt Lt Dunlop, the Officer in Charge. As he was all poshed up in his best uniform, ready to go off on a 48-hour pass, he was not best pleased at this turn of events. Needless to say everyone else thought it was hilarious. We got all the details from Peggy, who happened to be there at the time, when she popped down later to the Met Office for a reviving cup of coffee and dash of medicinal brandy. In her own words, when she thought her last moments had come, she saw her life pass before her eyes, and said goodbye to mother. This was the one and only time her smile was missing. It took a fright like that to make Peggy look solemn.

The Met Officers at Bourn were three – two married and one hoping to be. The senior, Flying Officer Jimmy Coutts, was married to a farmer's daughter and they were expecting an addition to the family at any moment. Second in command, Flying Officer Denis Stark, had a wife and baby in lodgings in Cambridge, and he it was who owned the BSA. The youngest, PO Paul Coleman was a tall youth whose fiancée had some frightfully important war job, and beside her all other females paled into insignificance. Paul didn't have a very high opinion of Waafs and constantly told us that his Diedre wouldn't dream of joining up and that no girls looked their best in uniform. This of course was a common point of view but none the less irritating because we were nearly all conscripted at this stage of the war and would have preferred to have been left alone to get on with our nice, comfortable civilian lives in peace. All three officers were, however, good meteorologists, having been in the Met Office in civilian life and put into uniform for convenience' sake. We were a happy unit, three men and five girls, and all got on well together, especially with Paul who, when he wasn't thinking about Diedre, was good fun to have around.

In the short summer nights of 1943, the battle of the Ruhr continued, and in July began the battle of Hamburg. From then until about March 1944, the going was very rough indeed and losses were heavy. Bomber Command's losses reached 5% per raid before the introduction of a radar jamming device known as 'window', the code name for strips of aluminium foil which the crews jettisoned from their aircraft when over Germany to confuse the night fighters. This did cut the losses for a while until the Germans devised a method of counteracting it. The Commander-in-Chief of Bomber Command, Air Marshal Arthur Harris, believed that his men were going to win the war, if necessary by themselves. It was believed that Butch, or Bomber Harris as they called him, didn't care how many men he lost if only the final result was the defeat of Hitler. The men spoke of him in genuinely affectionate terms, in spite of his nickname, and seemed to have great confidence in him. It was tough on the aircrews though, going out night after night to drop bombs on targets they couldn't see through the murk and the searchlights, but perhaps this very impersonality kept them going – that and the fact that they were young and usually had a few days between each mission when they could recuperate in the relative peace and tranquility of the English countryside.

Around the middle of August, we became aware that one very special operation was about to take place. Everything was very hush-hush, and it was not until it was over that the name of the target was made common knowledge – not that it would have been of any interest to us if we had known beforehand, because none of us had ever heard of it. Peenemunde. A lot of very senior RAF flying officers went on this particular raid, perhaps because it was too important and vital to allow young and inexperienced crews to take part. I don't know the reasons, I'm only guessing, but the fact remains that a group captain, no less, came over to Bourn from Huntingdon to attend our squadron's briefing, and then decided he wanted to go on the mission too. This was one night we were lucky and all our Lancasters came back safely.

Very often, even though the planes came back safely, there would be dead and injured on board, and sometimes a damaged aircraft would have been unable to release its bombs either over the target or in the North Sea on the way home and would have to land back at base with the bombs still on board. This could and did result in nasty crash landings which could set the bombs off. Whenever aircraft returned from raids the first persons to be allowed on board were the squadron armourers, whose job it was to make the bombs safe before anything else could be done, and this could be a highly tricky and dangerous undertaking, especially where incendiary bombs or those with time delay devices were concerned. Returning aircraft always had their own ground crews waiting on the airfield ready to assist in case of trouble, and relations between air and ground crews were of the highest possible standard. After the war, Bomber Harris tried to get an issue of a campaign medal for the ground crews on operational airfields, as he maintained they were completely ignored when the medals were handed out. In this I am afraid he was unsuccessful.

Pathfinder crews were lucky in several ways. They were usually first on the spot on a mission, so were often able to get away before the enemy night fighters were fully aware of the situation, and also, as they carried target indicators and markers, their heavy bomb load was consequently reduced. The so-called Main Force bombers from 5 and 6 Groups further north were usually later on the scene and were very heavily loaded with high explosives and incendiaries, and they came in for some real pastings. We heard that the Lincolnshire and Yorkshire stations lost far more men and aircraft than we did, and there was also a horrible story going around of an unfortunate rear gunner trapped in his turret as his plane landed, unable to get out and being roasted alive in full view of the ground crew, until a Wing Commander whipped out his revolver and shot him.

I used to think that an operational bomber aerodrome was the nearest thing to a front line, now that the blitz on London and other cities had eased off. Sometimes the German fighters followed the bombers back to their bases, and then when they saw the flare path light up for a few brief moments to guide the homecoming aircraft down, they would open up with their guns. It must have been the last straw to a tired Lancaster crew to have home in sight, and then to be attacked by a fighter. It happened twice at Bourn to my knowledge – once the fighter was shot down by anti-aircraft fire and the other time the rear gunner in the Lancaster was killed.

After a time I settled down into a routine of work, sleep and having a good time – and not necessarily in that order. None of us thought very deeply about anything. The war was on and it had to be won before life could become normal again. In the meantime, fun was to be had. There were the Station dances, the weekly cinema shows, and a superfluity of men. Always. As time went by, it seemed there had always been a war, and always would be.

5

'Long ago and far away'

We gradually got to know some of the members of our Pathfinder Squadron, and to realise that they were in fact rather special. The majority of them had completed one, and sometimes two tours of operations, and to have survived thus far was unusual when most crews rarely lived to complete a single tour. Most of them were now entitled to a ground job – 'flying a desk' – but they regarded this prospect with horror. I think they felt that having survived so far, they were now leading charmed lives and nothing could get them. As members of a Pathfinder Squadron they were allowed to wear a small brass albatross on their left breast pocket, immediately under their wings, and this was the only indication to anyone outside the RAF that they were in any way out of the ordinary.

Some of these men who passed through the Met Office were unforgettable characters. There was Sgt Steve Murdoch, a rough diamond of a Scot who broke all the rules by dating Sandy and an Intelligence Sergeant both at the same time – that is, on alternate nights. We used to pull his leg about this, asking him if he could remember which one it was tonight, and it goes without saving that the two girls were not even on nodding terms with each other. He had tremendous charm and needed it to get away with this. Then one night he went missing. The two girls were both on night duty and they waited in vain all night, hoping against hope that Steve and his crew had perhaps been forced down somewhere, but by the time dawn came up and there was still no news, they realised he was just another casualty. They passed each other in the corridor soon afterwards, and each could see that the other had been crying. I would like to record that they tried to cheer each other up in their double misery, but I'm afraid the truth is that as far as I know they never spoke to each other again.

One whom I shall never forget was a Canadian, the Station Navigation Officer, Wing Commander McMillin. Tall, prematurely grey, and I suppose in his early forties, he had a cheerful word for everyone and was adored by the whole camp, men and women alike. He came into the Met Office regularly and knew all our names. It seemed that he was extra attentive to me, and I heard via the grapevine that he always referred to me as 'the little Waaf with the starry eyes'. He had come unscathed through all his ops and then was reluctantly persuaded to become Navigation Officer, but he couldn't bear being grounded. Whenever any crew member was laid off sick, Mac was there taking his place. One day, a pilot named Flt Lt Mort had a sick navigator and Mac eagerly jumped into the gap, in spite of various people protesting to him that he must be mad to fly with a man who had a name like that. But it was all to no avail. Off he went with Mort, beaming happily, so delighted to be flying again, and yes – you've guessed it – Flt Lt Mort's plane was shot down in flames and no-one got out. Well, the whole camp went into mourning. It was as though we had all lost our favourite brother. There was a shadow hanging over Bourn for a time and nothing was fun any more. What was it all about when someone like Mac could be snuffed out, just like that? What was God doing up there – taking a nap? In the end, of course, we all pulled our socks up and got on with the job. What else could we do?

And then there was Glamour Boy himself, Flt Lt Eaton-Clark. He was the epitome of the dashing, flamboyant, slightly scruffy Bomber Pilot. His peaked cap was always bent at the most killing angle, his flying boots a bit dirty and his leather jacket perennially open. He gloried in looking a veteran flyer; the survivor of untold numbers of daring sorties. He was also very handsome and he knew it. He would come exuberantly into the office after ops with his crew tagging along behind him, to tell us that our weather forecast had been spot on, it had all been a piece of cake, bombs went down – Wham! – right on the target, no trouble at all, good show!, and here they were back on the old tarmac, cheating death again, etc. After which he would announce, 'Just going next door to ring up my Popsie!', and into the Signals Office he would disappear to ring up his fiancée, a Wren Officer stationed at Portsmouth. This of course was strictly against the rules, but such as Flt Lt Eaton-Clark did not bother about little things like that.

Later that year he and his Popsie were married in Cambridge, and there was a big spread in the local newspaper, with photos of him and his bride and some of his crew – from the neck upwards. (Pathfinders were still supposed to be something secret, and photos of that give-away gilt albatross were not allowed to appear in the Press.) So there they were grinning at us, six smiles above six necks – sorry, seven, I forgot about Popsie – and I cut it out and still have it somewhere. It seemed to me more and more as time passed that the RAF was bearing all the casualties of this war and that the other Services were taking life easily. Wrong, of course, but we were all so engrossed in this life that it was not possible until years afterwards to take an objective view. The boys went out night after night and some did not return. You picked up the pieces and went on. Come Hell or high water, the Met observations had to be made every hour, on the hour, and the show must go on. We didn't have the time or energy to pay much attention to the other theatres of war, unless we had someone out there. We were pleased when the news was good and depressed when it was bad, but first things came first and I suppose we all felt we were doing our bit and that our personal lives were at that moment of secondary importance.

Nevertheless, being normal healthy females we were always interested in the opposite sex and the general shortage of men in the country did not apply on bomber stations, where certain jobs such as Fitter, Armourer, Heavy Vehicle Driver, Electrician, and all occupations involving the handling of tools and machinery were still mainly considered the prerogative of men. The division was about four men to one woman, and this led to the inevitable result, in those days before The Pill – a baby boom. It is difficult to appreciate it now in the liberated 80's, but at the time the worst thing an unmarried girl could do was get pregnant, and the worst news a mother could hear from her daughter was, 'I'm going to have a baby!' At one point we had six expectant mothers in Hut 4, and only one was married.

Different people reacted in different ways. There was Scottie from Edinburgh, whose boyfriend was a navigator on a Lancaster called 'M' for Mother. He went missing one night when she was sleeping soundly across the hut from me, being under the mistaken impression that he and his crew had been grounded because of an electrical fault in their aircraft. The bad news reached her the next morning even before she had finished dressing, and then before very many days had passed she found out her condition, and the skies really fell in for her. She spent most of her time weeping and wailing to whoever would listen to her – and she really did go 'Boo-hoo!' exactly as it is written in the books. Her mother disowned her and she was sent, as was the custom then, to live out her pregnancy in a girls' hostel near Cambridge, doing housework for her keep. She was very wretched. I met her once on one of my off-duty bookshop prowls, took pity on her and gave her lunch. I suppose it was the least I could do. I was sorry for her, but in my opinion she had only herself to blame for being in such a mess, and I was smugly self-satisfied that the problems were hers and not mine. I really could not understand how a girl could allow herself to get into such a predicament. I was ignorant and had no worldly experience in those days.

Irene was different. She also was pregnant, but she bore her troubles with dignity and we all admired her very much. She had spent one night with her fiancé before he was posted overseas, and she was unlucky. (You'd think he might have been a *bit* more careful – after all, this wasn't happening in the Dark Ages before birth control was invented.) Irene had three much older spinster sisters who adored her, and her one consolation when she was discharged from the Waaf was that she had somewhere to go and three loving sisters to look after her.

For light relief we had Valerie, and why she didn't end up in the same boat I'll never know. The man in her life was called Illtyd, and he was a farmer in Wales who, because of his occupation, was not liable for call-up. He paid regular visits to Cambridge to see Valerie, and she would return to camp from these visits absolutely dying to pour out all her troubles to somebody, and as her bed was right next to mine it was usually me who had the honour. I think Illtyd was proving difficult to lead to the altar. At any rate, when I saw her approaching late at night from the last bus, I would feign sleep and lie rigid in bed, willing my eyes to stay shut, but the sagging weight of Val sitting on the edge of my bed and her heart-rending sighs usually wore me down in the end, and I had to open my eyes and listen. I always had the feeling that if I hadn't, she would have sat there all night. To this day, I can see Valerie heaving a deep sigh and murmuring in a piercing whisper which echoed all round the hut, 'I think I'm *ripe* for marriage!' Well, in the end the inevitable happened – Illtyd got fed up and called off the engagement, and thereafter 'Jilted by Illtyd' became a byword in Hut 4.

But most of us skated round these problems and didn't let ourselves become too entangled with anyone. There was certainly never a dull moment in our section of the Waafery. Nights were never very peaceful. There was always someone going on or coming off night duty, or reeling in late after a hectic night in the village pub. There was one never-to-be-forgotten occasion when one of the girls, slightly the worse for wear, staggered in and, evidently in dire straits, spent a penny in the fire bucket which was kept brim full of water in the middle of the hut. There was a predictable amount of uproar after that episode. Thereafter, we always made a point of asking the culprit, whenever we wanted to use the bucket for anything from watering the flowers to doing the ironing, 'Is this water in here or urine?'

Another girl, Sally Harcourt, was absolutely horrified at some of the things that happened. She was from a very high-class family. I considered I had had a sheltered upbringing – perhaps 'genteel' is nearer the mark – but she came from the world of country weekends, day and night nurseries, nannies, and never having to worry about where next week's housekeeping money was coming from, or having to do the washing up. I suppose she was the sort who would normally have been commissioned, but, all credit to her, she opted for the ranks and she was certainly finding out how the other half lived. She often used to say she couldn't believe how some people behaved, and the promiscuity and drinking shook her to the core.

Once we had a girl who never, but never, took a bath, and after suffering her proximity for far too long we made a complaint to Miss Malley. She came along, wearing gloves, and turned out the girl's kitbag onto the floor. The contents were immediately consigned to the rubbish tip and the girl forcibly removed in the direction of the bath huts. I am pleased to say she was afterwards housed elsewhere.

In the main it was a fun time for us girls. During the summer months it was pleasant to live in the gentle East Anglian countryside, to cycle around the small villages and to sunbathe when the weather permitted. Looking back, I seem to recall that summer of 1943 as a continuation of cloudless days and warm sunshine, with long pink and purple evenings filled with the roar and drone of aircraft taking off all round us. The night skies were star-filled and clear, the only snag as far as we were concerned being the dawn mist which appeared as the sky lightened and the squadron started to return, making visibility difficult to judge, both for us and the aircraft trying to land. I suppose there must have been the usual quota of cold, wet and windy days but I can't remember them.

One thing I do remember was an occasion when the occupants of Hut 4 provided the whole camp, unwittingly, with a topic of conversation which went the rounds for at least a week. Our hut was on the far side of the Waaf site and well screened by hedges and trees from the road which ran up the hill through the camp. At least we thought it was. But it was evidently not well screened enough, as we discovered one hot day when we were placidly sunbathing in our undies (Waaf issue, flesh pink and substantial). Six or seven of us were spread out on the grass toasting ourselves when we gradually became aware of a small knot of people gazing at us from across the field through a gap in the hedge, a knot which grew steadily larger all the time. It was borne upon us pretty quickly that the interested watchers were wearing air force blue, and that from the distance it probably looked to them as if we were all stark naked. It caused quite a sensation in the camp and people were flocking down from far and wide to have a good view, so we were informed later. I can just imagine it, 'Hey, have you heard? Nude sunbathing down on the Waaf site!' and everyone racing down to have a look. Luckily Miss Malley was on leave at the time, otherwise this event might just have been too much for her.

Occasionally, two or three of us off-duty would cycle down to the village on the long evenings of summer (winter was always difficult because of the chronic shortage of bicycle lamps). Once I went down with Jane to the village pub and we sat in the front parlour on our own, listening to what seemed to be a male voice choir performing in the next room, accompanied by mysterious foot shufflings and stampings. After a short while we couldn't stand it any longer; we had to find out what was going on. In the adjoining wall, strangely enough, there was a window with a curtain across it, so we pulled this aside to look and there were all these men dancing and singing and wearing horns on their heads. They looked furious when they saw our faces peering in and made frantic signs for us to close the curtains again. With the mystery unsolved, we finished our drinks and left, wondering if we had perhaps by chance witnessed some peculiar fertility rites which women were not supposed to know about. It was not until years later that I heard about the societies known as Buffaloes and Foresters.

Station dances were always well attended and a good time was had by all. On one memorable occasion, Mac came to one of the dances and spent a lot of time with me, even escorting me back to the Waaf site afterwards, making intelligent conversation about his home in Canada and shaking hands gravely as he said goodnight – so different from the smash and grab tactics I was usually treated to when trying to bring an evening to a satisfactory close. I'm afraid I didn't come out too well on this particular evening. I was so over-awed by the fact that he had sought out my company, that I was practically speechless. He was probably only being kind – he was kind to everyone.

One popular tune of this period will always remind me of Bourn, 'Long ago and far away.' It was played incessantly on the radio and at least once at every dance I went to, and the haunting melody was nearly always in my mind. For years afterwards I only had to hear it played and in my mind I would be back on the muddy camp site, feeling again the excitement and fun and tragedy which filled the air.

Towards the end of that summer, changes began to occur in the Met Office. First Sandy was posted to one of the other satellite airfields of 8 Group – I think it was Upwood. She was glad to get away for a change of scene, as it had just been confirmed that Steve had been killed, and her place was taken by Nancy, a tall, dark Scots girl, who fitted into the Met team very well. Nancy always proclaimed that the only man in her life was her father, who wrote to her faithfully every Sunday, 'My best boy friend', she called him. In spite of that, when an invitation was issued to all the Waafs at Bourn to attend an all-ranks dance and supper at another of the airfields near us, Oakington, Nancy didn't hang back when we were asked to put our names on a list of those interested in going. In the end three of us went, Mary, Nancy and I, the other two unfortunates having to work. There was a great deal of excitement while we were getting ready. When you all have to wear the same uniform, there isn't a great deal you can do to make yourself stand out from the crowd, but we did our best, washing and setting each other's hair and sharing out what precious bits of make-up we owned. For the first time in my life, my hair behaved itself and curled round my face in a manner which I considered most flattering, and my make-up went on well on a skin which didn't have one spot or blemish. As we set out in the truck which was going to take us the eight miles to Oakington, I was conscious that for once I was really looking my absolute best.

And I did have a splendid evening, spending most of the time with a red haired sergeant who seemed to appreciate my sense of humour – in fact, I thought we were getting on so well that I was disappointed when the evening ended and he didn't make any arrangements to see me again.

But the *big* success of the evening was Freda's – she ended up by getting engaged to a Flying Officer navigator whom she had never set eyes on until that night. That was the evening the Navy really got the elbow. It was a whirlwind romance, all right, and nobody could talk any sense into Freda. They didn't want to wait, either of them, and the wedding was arranged for the middle of October. The rest of us put our heads together to see if we couldn't all manage to get to it at Staines in Middlesex. The only way was to persuade one of the Met Officers to take over the observations and chart plotting for the day, and then we would all be back for the night duty. Jimmy and Denis we decided would not look too kindly on our request, the one being too staid and the other too much engrossed in his wife and family. So I was delegated to broach the subject with Paul Coleman.

When I diffidently approached him one afternoon, he

was, as usual, mooning over a photograph of the troublesome Diedre, whom we all knew from the pictures he constantly thrust under our noses to be extremely good-looking, and whom we suspected of being a bit of a girl on the quiet. It was unfortunate that at this period he was going through a protracted quarrel-by-letter with her and was generally grumpy and morose, especially if he had recently received one of her periodic letters informing him that it was *ALL OFF!* However, I said I would try so I put on my best uniform, nicely pressed, and as I paraded in front of him I said I had turned up the hem of my skirt and did he think it was too short? He gave me a sour look and growled, 'The whole thing's too short, from the head down!' (Diedre, of course, was tall and willowy.) This didn't bode too well for our hopes. I tried again, saying we were trying to decide how many of us could get to this wedding and we wanted to look smart, but the only response was that he didn't want to hear anything about weddings, thank you. That avenue was obviously closed to us and there was nothing for it but to go en masse to Jimmy Coutts and lay our case before him. The upshot was that after much argument all three of them agreed to help out, and all five of us did manage to get to the church on time. And the bride looked beautiful.

As a postscript to this, Paul's wedding did finally come to pass. He eventually got the girl to agree to a date and walked around with an idiot smile on his face for the few weeks beforehand. Later, he sent us a postcard from his honeymoon in Llandudno, penned in his schoolboy hand with the words, 'Having a MARVELLOUS time!'

Then in November began the Battle of Berlin. Bomber Command lost over 500 aircraft during the next few months over Berlin, and when you consider that this meant 3,500 fully trained men, it can be realised that it was a critical time. The Pathfinder squadrons continued to go first and drop their markers, but were not helped by unexpectedly adverse weather conditions over the target area. Lancaster crews hated going to Berlin. It was simply too far and too spread out. It was well beyond the range of the 'oboe' radar equipment and meant that they were wide open to fighter attacks as they approached the city. All through the winter the nightmare went on, through the worst of the weather – icing, snow, poor visibility. The crews were numbed with the cold in spite of their heated flying suits, and in these conditions it was all too easy to make mistakes.

Before a Berlin run the crews were always very subdued, and when they came back they were exhausted – *if* they came back. During this period, the American 8th Air Force squadrons of Flying Fortresses and Liberators, many of whom were stationed near to us in the vicinity of Cambridge and Huntingdon, were doing daylight raids deep into Germany, and were rapidly finding out that it was not as easy as they had expected. October 1943, was a terrible month for the Americans, when they lost roughly a third of their bomber aircraft, crippled or destroyed by the German Luftwaffe or ground defences. They quickly discovered that daylight bombing without fighter escorts was not on, and were also surprised to find that the RAF Lancaster was at least as formidable a fighting weapon as any of their own aircraft. Plodding away on the ground with our instruments and synoptic charts, we were not really aware of the significance and desperation of the events taking place in the skies over western Europe. Neither did we know anything of the controversy at high levels over the relative merits of area versus precision bombing, but what we did notice was that during the winter of 1943/44, morale amongst the aircrews was not exactly at its highest level. They were becoming very tired, and when they came back from their missions there was none of the former exuberance if everyone returned safely, and just fatalistic shoulder-shrugging if someone was lost. You bought it or you didn't.

The night of December 16th 1943, became known as Black Thursday, because a real pea-soup fog descended on eastern England while the squadrons were out, so that they came back to find every airfield shrouded in gloom and had to land all over the place. One of the 8 Group airfields, I think it was Graveley, had had FIDO burners installed along each side of the main runway – that is, 'Fog Intensive Dispersal Operation' – consisting of pipelines of oil which were lit up in foggy conditions. The flames did help to disperse the fog and also to make the runway more visible, but of course one airfield couldn't hope to cope with all the 8 Group heavies returning at the same time, and things were pretty chaotic for a few hours.

Somewhere about this time the squadron we had at Bourn was shifted up north to another Group. It created quite a stir on the camp when they left, as it was decided they would take all their ground crews with them in gliders. Those of the ground crews that we spoke to were not at all enthusiastic about this mode of travel – in fact a lot of them took an extremely dim view of it. They weren't air crew, for God's sake, they didn't join up to *fly*. To those of us standing on the sidelines, with our feet planted firmly on the ground, the manner of their going was quite exciting. As each plane took off with a glider following on behind, attached by a long rope, we stood watching from the Met Office in an agony of apprehension until each one was airborne. They all managed to get off safely, but we did hear that there were one or two very heavy landings when they arrived at their destinations. We assumed it was a practice for the invasion of Europe, which *must* happen sometime, and as such it was no doubt a valuable experience.

In the early months of 1944, Bomber Command losses hit an all-time high. In order for the crews to have a chance of completing a tour of thirty operations, losses had to fall below 4%, but on trips to Berlin, Stettin, Magdeburg and Nuremburg – all long-haul destinations – they sometimes touched 10%. It was a no-win situation for the unfortunate air crews taking part, and it would have been understandable if morale had completely cracked at that time. I like to think that we in the Met Office did our little bit towards keeping up the boys' spirits. More than one of them remarked on how pleasant it was to return to base in the early hours, cold, cramped and tired out, to see our welcoming smiles as they called in at the office on their way down to the Mess, even though they had probably only called in to tear us off a strip for having given them a rotten weather forecast.

During the three winter months, almost the entire squadron changed – well-known faces gradually disappearing and being replaced by new ones. It had a demoralising effect on us, and we wondered how long this could go on. Panic was kept at bay simply because we were too tired to think. We did our jobs, we fell into bed exhausted, and in our off-duty moments we got away from the camp as much as possible. One day, Jimmy Coutts cycled in to work (he 'lived out' with his wife and young family in a village near Cambridge), and said that he had seen a telegraph boy delivering a telegram at a house opposite his, where he knew the wife of one of the air crew officers at Oakington lived. 'The boy waited ages at the open front door after he had delivered it,' he said, 'but eventually he just rode away.' We all knew what had happened. Another young wife widowed, probably sitting in the kitchen too stunned to move. This dread of receiving a telegram was something our parents knew all about from the First World War, and here was history repeating itself. We couldn't do a thing about it, only get on with our jobs, living from day to day and, being young, looking forward to the day – surely not *too* far ahead – when things would start moving in our favour again.

Then, in the early spring of 1944, strong rumours began to circulate that big changes were coming to Bourn. The news broke that we were to have another squadron of Pathfinders, but these were going to be crack troops flying Mosquitoes, a much smaller aircraft than the good old faithful Lancaster, and much faster. We awaited their arrival with much curiosity, and on the morning of March 23rd 1944, as I cycled up the hill to work, the new aircraft started to arrive, 'beating up' the airfield to make sure we were aware that 105 Squadron was here. They were small, twin-engined planes which, as they circled and landed, looked so tiny next to the hulking great Lancs.

The 'Wooden Wonders' had arrived.

6

'The invasion has begun'

Mosquito crews were different, as we soon found out. There were only two men to an aircraft, and like a lot of Pathfinders they had nearly all survived two tours of operations. Their aircraft was also in a class of its own, being small and very nippy. They were the cream and they knew it.

Mosquitos rarely came to grief. They could fly above the flak and outstrip most German fighters. It was seldom that there was an aircraft missing after a raid, so gone were the days of losing seven familiar faces two or three times a week. They flew out fast, located the target with the aid of their radar equipment, dropped their coloured indicators to show the heavy boys where to go, and then nipped smartly back to base. Although made almost entirely of wood and having to land at what was then the extremely high speed of 100mph, I can only remember one incident of a Mosquito crashing and burning on the airfield. This occurred on take-off one evening and I happened to be in the Met Office at the time. We could see the burning kite about half a mile away, and the blood wagon and fire engine racing to the rescue. Naturally the rest of take-off was temporarily halted while everyone prepared to duck under anything convenient if the bombs exploded. I don't know why they didn't. A young pilot officer came into the office, white faced, and said to me, because I was on hand, 'That's my friend out there!' We gave him a cup of coffee and made soothing noises, but once again there was nothing we could do. The fires were soon put out, but both pilot and navigator were killed.

However, this was a rarity. Most times the squadron took off and returned safely, and gradually the life at Bourn changed. 97 Squadron of Lancasters left us at the end of April to return to Coningsby in Lincolnshire, from whence they had come, and with the loss of life drastically cut down, some of the pressure and sadness lifted, to be replaced by pressure of a different kind.

As 1944 got under way, rumours of the imminence of an Allied invasion of Europe grew. About three months before the actual event took place all leave was cancelled, even 24 hour passes, and Bomber Command was operational nearly every night, bad weather or good. We guessed what it was all leading up to but the exact date was a very well kept secret. Once the leave ban came down, our main method of relaxation on days off was to go into Cambridge. Everyone was feeling the strain of waiting, always waiting, for the action to start, and night duty on quiet nights – that is, when the weather was really impossible and all squadrons were stood down – began to be a real pain. Personally, by the time I had cycled up the hill in the dark, battling against high winds and rain, wearing my rain cape in a futile attempts to keep dry, I felt more like flopping into bed than sitting up all night making silly marks on a chart and plunging outside every sixty minutes to see if it was still raining. I used to think that we Met girls were the only ones awake and having to brave the elements. The worst thing was having to climb that damned ladder to the roof of Flying Control in a howling gale and lashing rain, to see how far I couldn't see across the airfield and to estimate the strength of the wind which was doing its best to dislodge my desperate hold on the railing. It all seemed a bit pointless – and anyway no-one but a raving lunatic was going to attempt to get airborne in those conditions. And I didn't feel very kindly towards the Duty Flying Officer and his mates asleep inside the Control Office. Many's the time I've slipped from top to bottom of the ladder, making a noise like the crack of doom, which was not however, sufficient to wake them (as I could tell by their uninterrupted snores). Lucky old them, they had nothing to do when the squadron was grounded.

The most scary task of all was on nights of thick, low cloud when we had to use the cloud searchlight, located on the far side of the airfield, to work out the cloud height. It was incredibly eerie to stand outside the office in the pitch dark, to press a switch and immediately have the whole airfield illuminated by the ghostly glow of this small searchlight, making its little patch of light on the cloud above. I was always much relieved to return to the light and warmth of the office.

To go into Cambridge at this time on our brief off-duty periods was really a life-saver and I used to go whenever I could, very often alone.

It was always a shock to me to find the life of the University town going along normally, as though the war was happening somewhere else. Students were everywhere, on bicycles, on foot, gowns blowing in the wind, most of them I suppose cramming in as much of their studies as they could before call-up. We didn't mix – the Forces and the students – as we really had nothing in common, but it was a reassurance to see them going about their daily business, as an indication that one day we would all be able to revert to peacetime pursuits.

Cambridge, like all University towns, consisted mainly of colleges and bookshops – and also bicycles. With the town being so flat, there were more bicycles than I've seen anywhere else except Holland. At each traffic light as the lights turned green, a mass of cyclists would be the first away, with cars, buses, etc, following on behind. Petrol was so strictly rationed in wartime that bikes were always in demand. Sometimes I cycled in from Bourn, but the eight miles all uphill on the return was a bit off-putting. Usually I caught the bus, and then returned in the evening on one of the several RAF trucks laid on for our use.

I spent a lot of time discovering and browsing through the bookshops, and then reading on the lawns which led down to the river Cam from the backs of the colleges. Mostly one was left in peace, as the sight of a solitary figure reclining on the grass, nose in book, was not one to encourage conversation. The only people who dared to interrupt were the American Forces, our valiant Allies, off-duty from the many American Air Bases in the area.

I had not at that time met any Americans but the sight of them prowling through what was now my favourite town, talking in their unfamiliar accents to anyone who would listen, rubbed me up the wrong way. After four and a half years of war involving food and clothes rationing, and bombing, and losing friends, the sight of these large, prosperous, untouched-by-anything foreigners parading round the streets, chatting up anything in skirts, was profoundly irritating. I think to a lot of us they were a big puzzle. In the first place, it was difficult to distinguish between the officers and the men. With our own Forces, the difference was immediately apparent in the quality and cut of the uniform, but the American uniforms all seemed to be very similar both in cut and material. But then to us they all had the same accent – they were just Yanks, chewing gum, blocking our paths

Leather goods and fancy goods.

Cedric and fellow airmen on Blackpool sands 1941. All RAF incoming airmen spent three weeks at Blackpool for drilling or 'square-bashing', while Waafs did the same at nearby Morecombe – and the twain never met!

(*Above left*) Cedric in airmen's uniform, Cambridge 1942, (*above right*) Three Waafs at Huntingdon – Rosie on the right, Olive in the middle. (*Below*) A Lancaster at Bourn 1943, with signatures of the crew.

(Above left) Aircraftwoman Second Class 1943. *(Above right)* My brother 1944. *(Below)* Binbrook May 1946. Left to right – Marjorie, Dora, self.

Squadron Leader Eaton Clarke's wedding. Eaton Clarke second from left, followed by his wife, Flt Lt Carlton and Sqdn Ldr Alabaster. The remaining three men were part of E C's crew. This newspaper photo was cut off under the chin for security reasons, so that the brass Pathfinder brooch was not shown.

The Waaf parade, Thanksgiving Sunday May 1945.

wherever we went, aggravatingly sure of themselves and their instant appeal to all females who hadn't actually got one foot in the grave. Of course, I realise I am being unfair and that they were mostly awfully lonely boys far from home. Many years later when I first visited the States I began to understand a bit of how they felt, as I too was then in an alien land – and make no mistake, America *is* an alien land, for all that we share a language and many common roots. The popular view of the Yanks of course was that they were 'over paid, over sexed and over here', and that about sums it up. And their uniforms were too tight.

Nevertheless, many girls found them attractive. They were highly visible, had plenty of money, and great numbers of British troops were then far away on distant battlegrounds. The girls they left behind had need of a bit of relaxation now and then. Looking back, I need not have turned my nose up with such scorn when any of them approached me, as I'm sure they did need some friendly contacts, but if one showed any signs of friendliness, they interpreted this as an invitation to attach themselves to you for the rest of the day, and probably the night too. I suppose the truth was we didn't understand each other. Our traditional British reserve made them think we were very hostile and resented them being here, and their extrovert camaraderie we regarded as showing off. It was true if you had an American boyfriend you stood to gain quite a bit in material goods, as their PX always seemed to be well stocked with food and silk stockings, cigarettes and make-up – all things in short supply in England – and for this reason if nothing else the Yanks were never short of female company.

My mother, having been deprived of one prospective son-in-law, Cedric, now got it in to her head that I might meet an American, and decide to marry him and live the rest of my life in the USA, where she couldn't get at me and see what was going on. This was before the days of relatively cheap air flights – in fact such things weren't even thought of by the bulk of the population. I was, however, able to reassure her on this point, as I could see no prospects of my ever getting close enough to any American for him to even ask my name, never mind ask me to marry him – and in the 1940's you *did* have to wait to be asked.

Around this time, Spring 1944, we had a re-shuffle in the Met Office. Wherever you were stationed postings tended to come out of the blue, and you would quite often arrive back from leave to find that in your absence you had been posted elsewhere. This happened to our Corporal Jane, who arrived back in camp after a brief visit to one of the neighbouring airfields to find that she had been posted to the Met Office at Group Headquarters, Huntingdon, and the corporal there, Rosemary Hilton, had received a reciprocal posting to Bourn. Jane departed in floods of tears and Rosemary duly arrived, in a very bad temper. She had been perfectly happy at Group. She had a boyfriend on an American station just outside Huntingdon, and it didn't suit her book at all to be shifted. *She* wasn't going to rot on any bloody out-station. While she hadn't actually been demoted, she felt she had been moved sideways, possibly because word had drifted through to those in authority who controlled our movements that the American already had a wife and children in the States. Maybe it was hoped that this move would cool the situation a bit. Who knows? But whatever the reason behind it, if there *was* a reason and it wasn't simply someone shaking up names in a box and picking one out here and there, it was like banging your head against a brick wall to attempt to fight against Movement Orders – here she was and she had to make the best of it.

Which she did very quickly, being a sensible girl. I got on well with Rosemary right from the start, soon realising that though I had lost one friend, I had found another. She was a very pretty girl and made her presence felt almost at once. As well as being pretty – tall, with auburn hair cut very short and smooth and classical features – she was keen and interested in her work, and when we were extra busy she would pitch in and help without being asked. She would come back to camp after a day off, call in at the office to see what was going on, and if we were all running around like headless chickens, snowed under with miles of paper from the teleprinter, and an irate Wing CO was tearing his hair out because the visibility had suddenly slumped from three miles to fifty yards and all his boys were up there somewhere running out of fuel, Rosemary would calmly take over the plotting while one of us rushed out to the screen to read the instruments, or go into the screaming teleprinter to shut off the insistent ear-piercing bell which was reminding everybody within hearing that we were late in sending in the hourly observation.

Once she came in about 4pm when I was on duty, face glowing from the blustery west wind, and said eagerly, 'I see the flare path's all lit up. Have we got ops on?' We had indeed, and Denis was in a filthy mood because his motorbike had died on him on the way into Cambridge and he had had to push it five miles back – and he had been taking his temper out on me ever since lunchtime. The weather was being at its most uncooperative – it was tippling down with rain when according to his forecast at briefing it should have cleared hours ago, and every single one of the navigators flying that night had been in to complain bitterly. Thankfully, I handed over my pens to Rosemary so that she could finish plotting the latest chart, and escaped outside for a few breaths of fresh air. And by the time I came back she had started the smoothing-down process that she was so good at. Rosemary was a friend indeed, and you could always rely on her.

The air crews used to flock around the office even more now that she was with us, and in particular a navigator called Henry who made numerous attempts to date her. Rosemary, playing safe, refused to go out with him unless I came too so in the end we used to make up a foursome with Henry's pilot, Jimmy, and with me sticking to my policy of not getting involved. (This policy came badly unstuck later on.)

Henry and Jimmy were known around the squadron as Laurel and Hardy. Henry was large and jovial and partly bald, while Jimmy was small and rather lugubrious in appearance and hailed from Glasgow. They were really a couple of characters. The story goes that one dismal morning they were detailed to take their Mosquito, 'D' for Dog, up for testing, and as there had been quite a party in the Mess on the previous evening, neither was feeling in the best of moods as they trudged out to dispersal at the crack of dawn. They took off in total silence, toiling upwards through the murk, and at 5,000ft the aircraft broke out into brilliant sunshine and clear blue skies. They peered out, and then at each other's dour faces and bloodshot eyes, and Henry's cherubic face creased into a wide grin. 'Good morning!' he chirruped. 'Nice day!', in the style of Dickie Murdoch, the comedian in 'Much Binding in the Marsh', the radio programme which was very popular at the time. Even Jimmy's early morning blues were not proof against that, and they eventually arrived back at base in a much better humour than when they took off. Jimmy was always quiet, even speechless, before ops, but on his return he was a different person. He would burst into the office singing, and if I happened to be there he would rush over and ruffle my hair, and exclaim, 'Here she is, the wee lassie! Waiting on my return as usual!'

We had a succession of crazy evenings out. The boys knew all the local hostelries and Jimmy even owned a car, a rather wheezy Austin 7, which had certainly seen its best days but still managed to clank around the country lanes when petrol was available. It even took us into Cambridge a few times, but that was pushing it a bit – and once or twice we really had to. When we were all off-duty of an evening, Rosemary and I would get ourselves done up in our civvies (strictly forbidden), and with our greatcoats and hats on to fool the eagle eye of the duty NCO in the Waaf Picquet Post, totter down the drive to await the arrival of the boys in the car. This could be heard approaching from some distance off, owing to its lack of an exhaust pipe, and was known around the camp as the Green Devil because it had, once upon a time, been that colour all over, instead of just in places as now. In we would climb, rolling up hats and coats and flinging them onto the back seat. It was mostly the village pub at Bourn we went to, or the similar one at Great Gransden, where we would sit in front of the fire and have a few drinks, and Henry would try to get Rosemary into a corner.

Some evenings were more convivial than others. One I remember vividly was when we had all been celebrating someone's 21st birthday (how young we all were!). The lad in question had a very poor head for alcohol and he retired very early on – under the table, if I remember correctly – but the party continued successfully without him. On the drive back to camp we were all rather happy, Jimmy in the front driving with me half asleep in the passenger seat, and Henry and Rosemary behind. I was listening to the two in the back working their way through a typical RAF ditty with the repetitive chorus of, 'There's only one bar – BOO! But its five miles long – HOORAY!' when Henry suddenly looked out of the window, sat bolt upright and exclaimed, 'Hey, Jim, we're on the bloody pavement!' We were, too – at least, the two nearside wheels were, but being the middle of the night there was a fortunate scarcity of pedestrians, and we quickly got back onto the road without disaster. Jimmy apologised profusely, explaining, quite logically we thought, that he had temporarily had his eyes closed and had put the car into automatic pilot.

On another memorable night, coming home in a thick fog Jimmy got us completely lost. We were following a long, straight road in visibility of about twenty yards, all of us hanging out of the windows in a vain attempt to spot landmarks, when a ghostly figure loomed up, saluted, and announced in long-suffering tones, 'Excuse me sir, Mr Mills, you're on the main runway!'

Many were the midnight cocoa sessions Rosemary and I had, sitting on her bed in the corner of Hut 4, trying to sort out her love life. I had never met her American, but of course with my prejudices I *had* to be on Henry's side, and I was therefore not much help to her. No help at all, I should think – I once fell asleep while she was arguing the pros and cons of Henry versus Hank-from-Texas, and toppled onto the floor with a very loud crash which woke everyone up.

Around that time, April or May 1944, an odd thing happened. My brother, now himself in the RAF, turned up at the door of the Met Office one morning, announcing that he had been posted to Bourn. With all the RAF stations in England for him to be sent to, he had actually been sent to Bourn and was there for a couple of months. I don't think the RAF knew what to do with him. He had joined up as Air Crew, and for several weeks had walked around proudly with the white flash in his cap, denoting that he had been selected for flying. But something went wrong. Perhaps there were simply too many applicants at that time. When you are in the lower echelons of any service, you are left guessing a lot of the time. The decision makers don't confide in you. You do as you are told and hope to God that someone knows what they are doing. Anyway, he was told that he was no longer being considered for flying, and when he turned up at Bourn he was an ordinary AC2, with no flash in his cap, and was put on General Duties, which seemed to consist, most of the time, of cleaning out the ablutions. He was not the type to make a fuss as some people would have done, but he was very fed up about it. I felt very sorry that someone who was a partly trained civil engineer should have to waste his time sweeping floors and doing other such menial tasks, but that's how it was – he was one of the unlucky ones – or should I say lucky?

When I began to be seen around camp with a new face, I was subjected to a lot of nudging and winking from those who didn't know the facts, and people came up to me with knowing smiles on their faces, saying, 'I see you've got a new boyfriend! What's his name, then?'

'He's my brother,' I would reply, stony-faced.

This brought forth the usual gales of laughter and requests to pull the other one, stop having them on, etc. No-one wanted to believe the simple truth.

Meantime, the build-up to D-Day went on, and the strain of waiting began to tell. People got snappy, and nothing could compensate for the lack of leave. We wondered, out loud and quite often, what was going on and how long it was going on for, but by the end of May we knew that something was definitely in the wind. The squadrons were in a state of perpetual motion with ops first being on and then off, orders being issued and then countermanded, and the pressure and suspense built up until it was almost unbearable. The air crews were out nearly every night pounding the French ports and railway marshalling yards and the squadron ground staff were rushed off their feet, particularly those involved in preparing the aircraft for flying as instructions were changed so many times. The targets were frequently altered, bomb loads changed, keeping the armourers constantly on the run with bombs lying about all over the field. And the weather didn't help. A gigantic undertaking like the invasion of Europe needed at least a few days of good weather to give it a chance, and we appeared to be settled into a period of wind, rain and low cloud. Day by day went by and there was still no sign of clear skies. 'Flaming June', people muttered bitterly amid the cascades of rain, and the thought of the poor men who must be waiting to set out across the choppy Channel in their small boats to fight a bloody battle on the other side made me feel cold and sick.

Not that we had much time for feeling anything, we were so busy in the Met Office just then. Freda, the newly-wed, was pregnant, and this was messing up all our duty rosters.

I had arrived up at the office one morning to relieve Freda from night duty, and found her sitting up there looking pleased with herself and Jim looking solemn. She had had her pregnancy confirmed by the Medical Officer, who had decreed that she must henceforth do no more night duties. Well, fine for her but that meant that the rest of us had to share her night duties out amongst us, and in our present state of tension we were not giving three hearty cheers for extra work. We were weary and didn't spare a thought for how she must be feeling – sick in the mornings, with a husband flying all the time. To us it was one more thing to cope with. We were now doing 12-hour shifts – all day, followed by all night, then a day off to sleep, and the cycle starting all over again. We could only carry on like this for so long, and it all depended on how well we could sleep during the day. Sometimes we came off night duty too tired to sleep at all, jaded and depressed, because there seemed to be no end to the dreary round of working, eating and trying to sleep. It became too much trouble sometimes even to go to the Camp Cinema.

But the nights of June 5th/6th changed all this.

As it happened I was on night duty. Our Mosquito squadron had gone out to bomb one of the usual targets in western France and when they began to come back, the first crew to come into the Met Office told us the news,

'The invasion has begun! We saw the ships crossing the Channel on our way back – hundreds and hundreds of them!'

We were all struck dumb for the moment. We'd been expecting this news for so long that we were scarcely able to take it in, in fact we were fairly incredulous. But then each crew who came back confirmed that it was true. They'd all seen the armada crossing the water. And then the 7am BBC News announcement settled any remaining doubts we may have had.

Our next reaction was fear that the invasion would not succeed because of the unusually rough weather. For several weeks that fear remained at the back of our minds and we wondered what was behind the brief news bulletins which were issued, and whether the whole fateful adventure would be a success. But after a week or two it became evident that the various bridgeheads were being held and advances being made (at what cost we did not then know, but could only guess at), and that this was in fact the big event we had all been waiting for.

7

A small light at the end of the tunnel

Much has already been written about the Invasion of Europe and I am in no position to go into details of the actual event, but can only record how it affected us in Bomber Command.

The war began finally to make sense. This is what it was all about, to push the Germans back, mile by mile, no matter how long or what dreadful toll it might take, until they were safely confined behind their own boundaries again. It was like a shot in the arm for us, and our tiredness fell away. The RAF ground crews, the unsung heroes of this time, continued to work round the clock, the air crews seemed never to be out of their aeroplanes, and the rest of us waltzed through our duties with the exhilarating feeling that at last things were on the move in the right direction.

The Met Office, naturally, came in for its usual rounds of flak through the unpredictability of the English weather. We girls were only the workhorses really – we read the instruments, plotted the charts, made the tea and kept the office clean, and were not meant to be able to give a weather forecast. We were in the happy position of being able to pass the buck. When any aircrew came raging in to inform us that our optimistic prediction of clear, moonlit skies and baby cumulus had in fact turned out to be 10/10ths stratus on the deck, we were able to wave them airily in the direction of Messrs Coutts, Stark and Coleman and say, 'You'll have to talk to them!' The unfortunate Met Officers all over Bomber Command had plenty of explaining to do during that summer, as the weather was unusually bad. No matter how carefully they pointed out that areas of low pressure almost always bring rain and high winds and plenty of cloud, it didn't help at all when Station Commanders and Navigation Officers specifically wanted clear skies and good visibility over their targets. Both Bomber Command and the American Air Forces were concentrating on oil refineries and synthetic petroleum plants as well as the usual railway marshalling yards and arms factories all over France and western Germany in order to enable the invading armies to carry on advancing, but air losses were heavy. A certain amount of desperation began creeping in. We felt it too – there was so much to lose now. The invasion *mustn't* fail.

Recently books have been written querying the efficiency and use of Bomber Command aircraft in the night bombing of Germany, and asking whether it did help in the final defeat or whether in fact it made little difference. At the time the thought never entered our heads that there could be any doubt about this, and it is certain that the effect on morale throughout the country was tremendous, especially as for months at a time the war news from other parts of the world was usually bad. Admittedly, we on the ground were not the ones who put their lives in danger every night, but as far as the air crew were concerned it was a job they had volunteered to do and they did it willingly, believing that every effort counted in the long run. The odds, as they well knew, were against them finishing even one tour, but war is a horrible business and we all had to do the best we could in discouraging circumstances. When the long-awaited Invasion finally started, we were sure that the lives which had been lost were now going to be partly justified, because the boot was definitely on the other foot and the Germans had had it.

We now had the air crews coming back from low-level sorties over France and Belgium and reporting damage they had seen to docks and military installations, and, much more upsetting, roads thronged with refugees all trying to get away from the zones of fighting. This saddened us all, but I suppose it was inevitable, and reminded me of things I saw during the 1940 Blitz on London when living in the northern outskirts of the city but working near Hadley Wood, with weekly trips down to our offices at Kings Cross railway terminus. It is well-known that the Blitz started with the burning of the London docks, and that this created a blaze so fierce that you could almost read a newspaper at night eight miles away. (I know because I tried.) During the first few days of the Blitz I had to go to Kings Cross and there I saw whole streams of weary and frightened East Enders pouring through the station, intent only on getting away from the bombing with what bits and pieces of their belongings they had been able to salvage; with their small children crying and bewildered, and family pets bundled up in rugs or protesting loudly in makeshift cardboard boxes. It was a pitiful, unforgettable sight, and I sincerely hoped I would never have to witness anything like that again. So now when our crews came back from their missions and we heard snatches of their conversations about long lines of refugees, about cities being devastated, and miles and miles of fires, I remembered Kings Cross and could only feel pity for what these civilians were now enduring; French, Dutch, German or whatever. They were just people, like us.

Goering thought the Blitz would bring England to its knees and we would sue for an armistice. He was wrong there, having misjudged the mood of Londoners, because even those who were completely bombed out and had nothing except the clothes they stood up in, nearly all came back again when the bombing eased off and they could find a roof to cover them. The size of the city and the fact that it was so spread out, too, was a factor in its favour, it being almost impossible to flatten London with the HE and incendiary bombs of those days. What he also couldn't be expected to know (and thank goodness he didn't), was how much more morally devastating were the V1 and V2 buzz bombs and rockets when they started falling on London soon after D-Day.

Once the Invasion was well under way, we were allowed to go on leave again. I went home for a week at the end of July, just in time to see the beginning of this new menace, the V1 buzz bombs and I have to say they completely terrified me. I heard a noise one night, like several motorbikes roaring down the road, only it was coming from above, and as I looked out of the window there they were – three red exhausts in the sky, blinding along a parallel course a few feet above the roof tops. As I watched, one of the engines cut out and a few seconds later I heard and saw the explosion, two or three streets away. With my feet frozen to the floor, I followed the red lights in the sky until they both disappeared and the two loud bangs which followed signified that they too had come down heavily somewhere. I became aware that feet were scuttling down the stairs, and my father was bellowing from the regions below, 'For God's sake, come down!' My maternal grandmother was living with us at the time, it having been decided that her flat in Highgate should be closed down for the duration of the war, and she circulated between the homes of her son and three daughters so that she could be looked after. She was now down in our kitchen, being given brandy, followed by hot, sweet tea for shock (we all had some of this), and we all spent the rest of the night huddled together under the Morrison table shelter in the dining room. As for the V2s – if anything they were worse, as you didn't get any warning at all, just an almighty explosion. I really think it was the V2s which finished my poor old granny off. 'Oh, whatever was that?' she used to cry, sitting down with a thump on anything that was handy, whenever one of them exploded within hearing. They did some dreadful damage and caused a lot of loss of life. I believe it was a V2 which demolished the Guards' chapel in Knightsbridge during a service, killing dozens of men. Anyway, granny didn't survive the war – her heart gave out one night and there was a big family funeral to which I did not go, having conveniently arranged to be on duty that day. I'd had enough of people I knew dying or being killed, and I didn't want to be there to see all my relatives being miserable and to listen to their bomb stories.

Coming after five years of war, when for the first time there did seem to be a tiny light at the end of the tunnel, these new rockets were almost too much for our overstretched nerves, although the situation would no doubt have been very much worse if it had not been for the times when both the RAF and the American Air Force had been out bombing Peenemunde and the other rocket sites.

During that week of leave there was one other incident which was memorable and could have been serious, if not fatal, for me. One night when there was an air raid alert on, and we were trying in vain to sleep through the usual 'noises off', mainly the big anti-aircraft guns situated it seemed at the end of the garden, there was suddenly the most appalling crash immediately over our heads. We were downstairs, laid out like sardines under the Morrison shelter, but when this happened my Dad was up like a shot and racing up the stairs with a bucket of sand, ready to throw it over what we assumed was an incendiary bomb which had come through the roof. My mother and I helped push him up the ladder into the attic (not easy – he was no lightweight), and then passed up the bucket for him to quench the flames. But there were no flames. All was dark and silent up there. Much puzzled, we searched through the bedrooms, and there in my room we found the cause of the commotion. The nose-cone of one of our own anti-aircraft shells – still smoking – was reposing on the pillow of my bed, burning a neat hole in the pillow case and scorching the feathers. Much impressed with my narrow escape, Dad carried the object downstairs on top of the sand in the fire bucket – it did come in handy after all – and we sat around gazing at it, drinking the inevitable tea and storing up this tale to pass on to all our friends and relations. There was much competition during the war as to who could come up with the best bomb story, and my mother had a great time telling this one to all the aunties, especially as it was only due to her nagging that I hadn't been in my bed at the time. I didn't care to be squashed up in the shelter.

What we should have done of course, and didn't, was to notify the neighbours who were on fire-watching duty up and down our road. Everyone took turns to patrol the streets at night during air raids, and had to be particularly vigilant in the event of firebombs, because if they were on the spot with their fire buckets of sand and water, many a fire could be put out before it got too bad. On this night the fire-watchers heard the nose-cone come down, it made such a crash, thought it was an incendiary, and spent the rest of the night searching for it, in vain. My father wasn't too popular the next day when he told them what had happened.

One way and another, I was glad to get back to Bourn after this leave for a rest. Everyone said I looked worn out and must have been gadding about too much! Fat chance of that with all these things zooming about overhead. I was thankful that Cambridgeshire was pretty well out of reach of both V1s and V2s. We could hear the V2s thudding down onto London in the far distance, but the sound came over as a far-off double bang, which puzzled us for a long time until someone told us what it was.

As summer continued, life seemed to get a bit easier. Gradually the combined armies in France managed to gain more than a toehold on French soil and started to advance, and our aircrews found themselves flying over more and more territory which was in friendly hands, so therefore the casualty rate in Bomber Command dropped dramatically. Then, in August, Paris was liberated! That really was something to cheer about, and people started to go round saying it would all be over by Christmas. On the newsreels at the cinema we saw pictures of de Gaulle riding in triumph through the streets, swastikas being torn down, ecstatic Parisiennes in their un-bombed city kissing the troops and giving them flowers. Rockets were still falling on London, but Paris had been liberated so surely, *surely*, it was nearly all over?

Not so, of course. The Germans were not simply going to let us walk in. As far as the RAF was concerned, they had this nice little lull when losses fell substantially, so it was for us a calm period in the storm. Nights when ops were on were not so hectic now that the boys did not have the long runs to Berlin and Nuremburg, just specific targets in France and western Germany. Things would have been pleasanter if the weather had been more summery, but you can't have everything and in England one gets accustomed to wet and windy summers. We were able to get on with our routine work without too much drama unfolding around us, and we started to dream of what we would do when the war was over.

The day-to-day life of an RAF station went on as usual, no matter what was happening in the big world outside. Nancy, who had been in the Waaf two weeks longer than me, was recommended for her Corporal's stripes. She really deserved them but she never got them. Those of us who didn't join up until 1943, either because we were too young or like me in a reserved occupation, didn't really stand much chance of promotion, not unless we were absolutely brilliant and not many of us were that. The girls who had been in since the start of the war had cornered the market in stripes. All the Met Waafs at Bourn had by this time qualified for their 'props', so we were two steps up from the bottom of the ladder and that's where we stopped.

Someone tried to organise a concert party, and there was a great deal of enthusiasm for this for a short time. Anyone who could play an instrument or sing in tune was roped in, and I found my name put down on a list to be a chorus girl. Bob, the LAC electrician who was trying to get the show off the ground admitted that his main ambition after the war was to be the conductor of a classical orchestra. He didn't really mind which one, the Hallé would do for a start, but he hadn't the faintest idea how to go about it and nor had anyone else. His knowledge of classical music was very comprehensive – you only had to sing him a snatch of any symphony or concerto and he would be able to identify it immediately, but this isn't sufficient to get you up there in front of a hundred or more qualified musicians and be able to lead them into the opening bars of Beethoven's 5th, or even the Warsaw Concerto. Perhaps he thought that if he made a success of the concert party, word would get around amongst show business that here was someone to keep an eye on, and his big chance might come; that someone important in the music world might come up to him with a contract in his hand and sign him up for the next ten years as a successor to Sir Malcolm Sargeant. Well, I know pigs might fly, but hope springs eternal and Bob was eternally hopeful that something like this might happen.

However, the concert party folded before we had had more than a few ragged rehearsals, mainly because Bob's girlfriend, a tall, bossy Waaf who fancied herself as another Vera Lynn, suddenly went all narrow-minded and decreed that if there was to be a chorus line, we were not to show our legs but to wear slacks. Needless to say, she was not in the chorus as she had legs like inverted beer bottles. We were so incensed by her trying to run things just because she was Bob's girlfriend – after all, what's a concert party without a leg show? – that we left in a bunch, and that was the end of that idea.

One night we had a crash landing, when a plane from another airfield had to land at Bourn in a bit of a hurry, having been shot up rather badly on the way back from Germany. It finally came to rest near the caravan, at the start of the runway. During take-offs and landings, some Flying Control personnel would occupy a caravan placed near the start of the runway being used, and they would fire green or red flares to let the aircraft know if they were cleared to land or take-off, and on this occasion one of the men was very quick off the mark, saw the crash and was immediately on the spot, helping the crew to get out of the burning aircraft. For his pains he was highly commended and posted to another airfield on the east coast, one of several which were used exclusively by crippled aircraft limping home and unable to make base. At these airfields, crashes were the order of the day and I don't think this particular airman was any too pleased at this result of his unpremeditated heroic action.

One day during the early summer, Guy Gibson of Dam Busters fame flew in to Bourn and was with us for a few hours. One of the Intelligence Waafs was a relation of his, a cousin I think, and she was so proud of him. When he left, we watched from the Met Office windows as she stood at the salute on the edge of the perimeter track, until his aircraft was out of sight. It was so sad, as it wasn't very long after that he was reported missing, believed killed. He was, after all, a legend in his own lifetime, and now he was one more dead hero. It was one of the tragedies of wartime.

As the summer progressed into autumn, it became apparent that the days of strain and worry were far from over. The Arnhem debacle effectively put an end to our hopes of peace by Christmas, and gradually it seemed that the combined Allied armies were slithering to a halt. Our boys made intense efforts to back them up with air support, but were much hampered by consistently bad weather, and it soon became obvious that long supply lines and determined German resistance were combining to bog everyone down. I do remember clearly how depressed we became as the weeks went by and we could see, looming ahead, yet another wartime winter with its accompanying cold, damp and bad news.

Mary's fiancé, Johnny, who was a sergeant motor mechanic on one of the bomber airfields in Yorkshire, came down to visit her and took us all out for a drink one evening. He told us some harrowing stories of life on a bomber aerodrome which had 'main force' squadrons, always carrying heavy loads of high explosives and incendiaries, and impressed on us how lucky we were to be on a Pathfinder station. It did seem that the main force squadrons in other Groups had more casualties than we did, partly because they had to cope with fully awakened defences, gun and searchlight crews as well as fighters, after PFF had done their job, and perhaps also because they had a higher proportion of new, inexperienced crews who were usually the first to come to grief.

Towards the end of November 1944, or maybe the beginning of December, we had the usual succession of dark days before Christmas, made worse by thick, penetrating fog. This was before the Clean Air Act was passed and London smogs had to be breathed to be believed, but all the way up eastern England it was pretty bad. The milky-white substance which cloaked Bourn every day totally stopped the heavy bombers from taking off, and at that time the Allied armies were coping with the Battle of the Bulge in France and desperately needed air support. Eventually, on a day when the visibility at Bourn was about twenty yards, the powers-that-be decided that four Mosquitoes from our squadron would make the attempt to take-off for an undisclosed destination in France, each carrying a 4,000lb bomb. The bomb-bay of a Mosquito was too small to accommodate so large a bomb, and they had to carry them slung underneath the fuselage with the bomb doors open. The fog was too thick for any of the heavies to attempt take-off, but it was thought that the lighter, smaller and more manoeuverable Mosquitoes might just make it. The entire Met staff climbed up the ladder to the roof to check on the visibility – well, that's a laugh, we couldn't even see the runway, and I don't suppose the pilots could either. The situation at the other end must have been grave to warrant such an effort. It was really extremely hazardous, and as we stood there peering vainly into the blanket of fog it did cross my mind that we were all quite crazy. If one of those bombs went off prematurely we would all have been blown off the roof, and what good would that have done anyone? We could hear the engines revving up as one by one the aircraft started their nerve-wracking blind journey down the runway, and miraculously each managed a safe take-off without dislodging their bombs. We couldn't see the slightest movement in the fog, but gradually the noise of the engines diminished and died away, and the collective sigh of relief from the top of Flying Control must have had some part in the clearance of the fog, as by the time all four aircraft returned (bomb-less) we could acutally see the 1,000 yard marker on the other side of the field.

This was only a temporary relief, though. The fog came back over and over again that late autumn and early winter, and the dark days before Christmas that year were very dark indeed. The last and greatest battle of the Ruhr was fought in the skies over Germany in the last three months of 1944, and on some nights there were still 5% losses of aircraft, not to mention men. Bomber Command never overcame the problem of the weather, right to the bitter end, and right to the end the Germans fought back.

One really dismal day when the sky was totally covered by a dense grey blanket of cloud, the OC sent up one of the Mosquito pilots to find out the cloud depth. It started about 500 feet above the ground and could have continued all the way up to the stratosphere, for all any one of us, peering hopefully upwards, could tell. I was on day duty with Jimmy Coutts and I was peacefully plotting a chart on the far side of the chart table, which was hidden from the entry door by the screen which ran nearly the length of the room. Anyone entering from outside would only have seen Jim with his feet up in front of the fire, reading a thriller. In came Flt Lt Marshall, red faced and furious, having taken his plane all the way up to the top of the cloud and all the way down again. 'What's it like up there?' asked Jim.

'F---ing awful!' came the immediate reply.

There was a long silence – what I think might be called a pregnant pause.

Now I am well aware that times have changed and in

these more liberal-minded days such a remark might pass with only a raised eyebrow or two, but in 1944 men did not use four-letter swear words in front of girls, be they ever so lowly – and they didn't come much more lowly than we were. I didn't see why he should get away with it so I decided to make his day for him. I wandered round the end of the screen and sweetly asked him if he would like some coffee, and then watched the poor man's jaw drop and his face go turkey red. Jim thought this was priceless and laughed so loud and so long that he brought the Duty Officer down from Flying Control to find out what he'd missed. I've no doubt the joke went all round the Officer's Mess. Flt Lt Marshall was extremely embarrassed and always avoided my eye whenever he came into the Met Office after that.

Christmas loomed nearer and the news from France did not improve. Neither did the weather. Day after day we were fog-bound in East Anglia and all our aircraft were grounded. Henry and Jimmy went off on a 48 hour pass with a couple of nurses they had met at a dance in Cambridge, so, feeling decidedly sour, Rosemary and I went into Cambridge on our own on Christmas Eve. The Backs always attracted me, even in a winter fog, and we eventually found ourselves in King's College Chapel for what I think must have been the very first of the annual carol concerts. We were not feeling at all holy when we went in, having decided that all men were rotters, and fancy leaving us at *Christmas* for a couple of dames they had only just met!

But perhaps our feet were guided there, because we came out much soothed and at peace. Standing under the vaulted fan roof of that incredible building, listening to the pure soprano of the leading choir boy singing, 'Once in Royal David's city' as the choir came up the aisle, it was difficult to restrain our tears. Here we were, approaching the sixth wartime Christmas and still the end didn't seem to be in sight. Even if the Germans were at last being pushed back, there were still the Japanese to demolish, and they were no soft touch by all accounts.

Somehow, though, we did feel better as we filed out at the end of the service and made our way down to the river. The Cam always looks so peaceful, especially so on a winter's day with no punts or rowing boats in sight. Henry's defection to the charms of the nursing profession had finally made up Rosemary's mind for her, and from now on it was going to be Hank-from-Texas who occupied all her thoughts. Apparently he was getting a divorce, and Rosemary was already planning the wedding and her honeymoon trousseau – such as it would be in those days of strictly limited clothing coupons.

We wandered over Clare Bridge, which always looks as if it is about to collapse, and then up to St John's, where we stood on the old Wren bridge and talked for some time, gazing at the so-called Bridge of Sighs which connects the old and new parts of St John's. Rosemary had been to Venice and seen the original bridge, and she enthused for a long time on the beauties of that city and how much she would like to go there again after the war was over. I wondered how she would settle down in the United States when she and Hank did get married. America has natural beauty in abundance but is a bit short on architectural gems such as St Mark's or the Rialto.

After a while we decided to round off the day by taking ourselves to the cinema, and ended up by catching the 11pm liberty wagon back to camp.

That was a bitter winter in all ways. The weather was the worst for many years, and the news from the Continent as the advancing armies uncovered first one and then another of the German concentration camps was almost unbelievable and quite horrific. We had to believe the photographs which appeared in the newspapers, but I think we all asked ourselves how such things could be in a so-called civilised world.

The worst thing that happened to me was that I was moved to another hut on the Waaf site and found myself amongst a very superior set of girls who worked in Radar. Well, they *thought* they were superior because their trade was classified Grade 1 and Met was only Grade 2, so they got paid more than I did and considered they were a cut above me in every way. It nearly killed them to acknowledge my existence and they only spoke in monosyllables when I was present, but the babble of sound which broke out every time I went out and closed the door behind me was enough to make me want to go rushing straight to Miss Malley to beg her to send me back to my friends. I didn't, of course, but suffered in silence and considered myself a martyr.

There was a general feeling of change in the air. Mary was posted to a notorious station in the Fens, called Sledgwick, which was universally known as HMS *Sledgwick* because it was practically under water and everyone wore gumboots and walked about on duck-boards. She was much disgusted and sent us a postcard saying she was developing webbed feet.

I think we all accepted by now that we were going to win the war, and that this time there was not going to be an armistice but final defeat for Germany. It also meant constant fighting right up to the last day, and for Bomber Command no let-up in the night by night sorties into enemy skies. Gradually, as the armies pushed on through France, French airfields were taken over by the RAF and the Americans, and one day Jimmy and Henry were posted to a station near Rennes and that was the last we saw of them.

In early spring came my turn to be moved. I called in at the office on one of my days off, to see what was doing, and found that a posting had come through for me to report forthwith to Group Headquarters at Huntingdon. I received this piece of news with resignation but no enthusiasm. I'd heard all about Group from Rosemary and it didn't seem to be my sort of place. However, that was service life.

We had a bit of a party in the Met Office that night, tearful farewells were said all over the place, and I departed the next morning with my kit and a bad headache, ready for whatever Fate had in store for me.

8

Stop the plane, I want to get off!

I suppose I was overdue for a move. It seemed to be RAF policy to shift people around from time to time, usually just as they were beginning to take root somewhere. I had been at Bourn for two years and had seen many people come and go, but if I had had a choice I would not have chosen to go to Group Headquarters.

It was entirely different from being on an out-station. For one thing it was not an airfield but a large old house right in the centre of Huntingdon, a small market town about twenty miles west of Cambridge. In peacetime the town must have been a sleepy and slow-moving place, but at the start of 1945 it fairly hummed with activity, being surrounded in all directions by RAF and American Air Force stations. It was stiff with blue and brown uniforms, the blue being mostly Waafs and the brown American airmen, plus a few pasty-looking American girls – 'rejects' as they were unkindly called.

There were no aircraft or aircrew and the Met girls' sole job was plotting charts, a new one every hour, and collecting the teleprinter reports as they came in from each of the out-stations in the Group. Sometimes if there was a certain amount of urgency due to bad weather, or perhaps a very important operation, the observations were collected over the telephone link-up, with the Met Officer in charge listening in. Every station sent in the reports in code and we collected them and sent them on to Bomber Command Headquarters. It was very painstaking, eye-straining work, with all the extra plotting and without the alleviation of trotting outside each hour to scan the horizon and study the sky. Before I had been there a month my eyes began to suffer and I had to start wearing glasses for close work.

I must admit I missed seeing the aircrew boys around. The only men in evidence at Group were the Met and Operations Room Officers, and a few erks to do the pen-pushing jobs. These latter were nearly all middle-aged or C3 with bad eyesight, so the outlook was not exactly exhilarating.

Once we stepped outside the seclusion of our HQ, however, it was a different story – we had the American Air Force to deal with. Every time we ventured outdoors, we had to brave the ranks of these dozens of seemingly unoccupied Americans who would sit in lines on the low walls surrounding the house, wolf whistling and just waiting to pick up a girl. It didn't matter how ugly she was. She only had to have the usual amount of arms and legs and to be able to see where she was going. For any girl who was a little bit shy it was sheer agony to go out at all. The only way was to push straight ahead and try to ignore them. It was no use trying a friendly smile because you immediately developed a long line of followers and felt like a comet with a tail. The townfolk always stared as if we were doing it on purpose, and that made us feel worse.

I once watched a Yank pursuing a Waaf down the length of Woolworths in Cambridge. He was quite a personable young man, but the Waaf I recognised instantly as the one who had been ejected from Hut 4 at Bourn for being dirty. I knew she had no morals to speak of and would go out with anyone who had the price of a couple of drinks on him and wasn't too fussy about where he spent the night, and I thought these facts would surely be obvious to any casual passer-by. You only had to look at her greasy black hair, her insolent stare and her creased and spotted uniform. Couldn't he see that? Or didn't it matter? These Yanks were a puzzle to me.

One afternoon I went out with another girl for a walk, with the idea of finding a quiet spot in the meadow we called the Big Field, to read and write letters. We always went out in twos and threes, for obvious reasons, but all the same by the time we were approaching the field we had collected a following of about a dozen. After snarling a few choice remarks at them from the corners of our mouths, such as, 'Get lost!' or 'Beat it!', which we understood to be good American for, 'Please go away, we do not wish for company,' we managed to rid ourselves of a few of them, but two of the most persistent followed us until we were clear of the town, and then we realised that the only way to be left alone was for us to be really rude. Even after that, they still seemed to be completely bewildered, and kept repeating, 'But you don't really *want* to be alone, do you?'

I write now as I found at the time. It was the sheer effrontery, the excessive assurance of them which got under my skin. There must have been a proportion of shy, bashful ones around, but they were not in evidence amongst the mob which harassed us day by day as we tried to make our way around the town on our own affairs. I wondered if our own troops in distant countries behaved in this way. Somehow I couldn't see it – they didn't have as much money as the Americans for one thing, and that must have inhibited them considerably.

In any case, I like to think that their manners were not so coarse.

Back in the Met Office, for me it meant a completely new set of faces.

The Chief Met Officer, Wing Commander Thomas, or 'Tommy' as he was always called by us behind his back, was immensely popular but a strict disciplinarian. We always had to be properly dressed even in the wee small hours when we were only looking forward to being relieved so we could fall into bed. No sloppy out-station manners were tolerated at Group. We had to be neat and tidy with our ties properly tied, our shoes laced up, and he liked us to look wide-awake and busy even if we were not. One girl who turned up for night duty wearing plimsolls received a proper rocket. Occasionally Group Captain Bennett would poke his nose in to make sure everyone was getting on with the job and not larking about. There was a sense of importance, of being at the heart of things. To be at Group Headquarters at all one had to be competent – I think the Met girls who were chosen had to be very neat with their pens. I suppose it was promotion in a way.

There were six or seven Met Waafs, including a sergeant and two corporals, and the rest were LACWs like me. We were housed in the usual huts, but being this time in the centre of a town, we had paved paths all around us and shaded lights to help us get about at nights, and not having to go out at night to read instruments was a welcome change. Nevertheless, at first I was lonely and missed the free-and-easy atmosphere I had left behind, until I began to get to know people.

One of the easiest to get along with was Rosie Michelle, a small cheerful Cockney girl who was definitely in awe of no-one. She was no respecter of persons and never thought before she spoke. She was always slightly scruffy, while not actually dirty – I think 'off-white' describes her perfectly. I remember once when she was climbing into bed in her Waaf-issue blue striped pyjamas, a cheeky little field mouse popped up from between her sheets where it had evidently been nesting, and streaked across the hut to disappear down a convenient crack in the wooden wall. Those of us near enough to have observed this were by now climbing onto chairs and beds and squealing, 'It's a mouse!', but Rosie continued her progression into bed, pulled the clothes up to her nose and regarded us all with mild astonishment. It did not occur to her to strip her bed down and change the sheets, or even to pull them back to see if there were any more where that one came from. You couldn't help liking her – nothing fazed Rosie. She was only about five feet tall, thin and blonde with a bony London face, and her stick-like legs were not enhanced by the thick, grey Waaf stockings and flat lace-up shoes we all had to wear. You had to have legs like Marlene Dietrich to triumph over that get-up. She had an American boyfriend whom she was cultivating like mad and apparently he was so stunned by the first sight of Rosie's straight grey legs and black feet pointing to twenty past eight that he took several photos of them with his expensive Leica camera, exclaiming joyfully, 'Oh boy! I have to get a picture of those feet! They'll never believe this back home!'

Rosie's one ambition was to get to America, and the easiest way was to marry a Yank and become a GI bride. I don't know if she ever pulled it off.

However, when I had been in Huntingdon a few weeks she persuaded me, against my will, to accompany her to a dance which was being held at Alconbury, one of the American air bases nearest to us. I was instructed to leave my prejudices behind and simply concentrate on having a good time, so I set off with that one idea in mind. Several transports were sent to convey us to the camp, and they were certainly less basic than the RAF ones we were used to, and when we arrived at the aircraft hangar where the jollifications were being held, it was ablaze with coloured lights and swarming with people, and a seven piece band was being very loud on the platform. We also caught enticing glimpses of tables laden with food through an open doorway. I did enjoy myself, once I had accustomed myself to the way the Yanks danced. They had two ways – cheek to cheek for the 'smoochy' tunes, and jiving for the lively ones. I wasn't too keen on this cheek to cheek business, with men I'd never seen before and didn't know the names of, but I kept on telling myself not to be standoffish and to relax a bit, but as for jiving – no, I couldn't do that. There were a lot of civilian girls there, wearing short, flared skirts and matching pants, and to see the way the men swung the girls up under their arms and even over their heads was quite an eye-opener. They all seemed to be having a lot of fun, and I envied them, but the thought of jiving in a tight blue skirt and Waaf knickers was quite impossible. Even so, I noticed Rosie was doing it, and that was quite a sight too! We all had heaps to eat, particularly the ice cream which we hadn't seen since the war began, and came back to Huntingdon at midnight after a thoroughly enjoyable evening.

Other girls at Group included 'Jolly Molly' – plump and good-natured; Harriet, who was trying to improve her mind and always listened to the afternoon plays on BBC radio (relayed to each hut over the Tannoy system); Veronique, who was stage-mad and had a friend in the current London production of *Lady Windermere's Fan*, and dough-faced Olive (more about her a bit further on).

Then there was Teddy, corporal in charge of the General Duties office section. To see her at work during the day, with her hair pulled straight back and no make-up on, and to hear her ticking off her girls if they were slacking, you wouldn't dream it was the same girl who was out dancing with a different partner every night. Teddy all made up to go out was a cross between Ginger Rogers and Rita Hayworth – her red-gold hair a mass of curls, false eye-lashes long enough to sweep the streets, face entirely out of a box (courtesy of the American PX), and fully fashioned grey silk stockings which were strictly *not* Waaf issue. She even made the Waaf uniform look glamorous. Her boast was that she had been dancing at every RAF and American air force station within a 30-mile radius, and that she wouldn't look at any male with a rank lower than Squadron Leader or the American equivalent. We all envied Teddy her looks, her poise and her social success. The fact that she eventually settled down and married an insignificant LAC pay clerk there on the staff at Group is one of life's little mysteries. It just shows what love can do. The last time I saw Teddy was one morning shortly before I left Huntingdon for my next posting. The war was just over, and she was climbing aboard an RAF transport to take her to the demobilisation centre. She looked terrible, pale and yawning and strangely bare without her eyelashes. When someone remarked in surprise at the speed with which she had obtained her demobilisation, Teddy replied mildly in her soft voice, 'But I'm married, dear!'

Well, I wasn't married or likely to be, as far as I could see. I was eight months at Huntingdon, from February to October 1945, and during that time the war came to an end, first the German war and then, most unexpectedly, the Japanese war. Once VE Day was over, we were all very happy because it meant the end of air raids and bombing attacks on Germany, and we now turned our thoughts to the problem of subduing the little yellow perils. Then came Hiroshima and Nagasaki, and miraculously the whole things was over, instead of our having to face what would probably be a long naval and air war against Japan, which we should of course have won in the end – after unthinkable losses of men and equipment. No-one, except perhaps a few scientists, had any idea of the long-term effects the dropping of these two bombs would have on the unfortunate Japanese – and perhaps even the scientists were unsure.

I was on duty for both the VE and VJ nights so took no part in either celebration. It was marvellous that it was all over, but it took some time to sink in, and in any event had no immediate effect on most of us. The arrangements for demobilisation were based strictly on length of service, except for those girls who were married and they got out almost at once. I could see no prospects myself of being released in much under twelve months.

The life at PFF Headquarters went on much as before. We all went on doing the jobs we had been trained for. There didn't seem to be anything else to do. Now that we could relax a bit, we began to realise just how tired we all were and many girls came down with minor ailments, such as skin rashes and tonsilitis.

However, by this time a new interest had entered my life. In the huts where we lived, we each had a card pinned over our beds which announced our names, our Waaf occupation and our religion. For those of us who only went to church for weddings, christenings, funerals and compulsory church parades, it was usually C of E (Church of England). But I very soon noticed that, over the two beds nearest to mine, was the highly interesting word 'spiritualist'. Interesting to me, that is, because my only previous contact with the world of spirits had been an eerie couple of evenings spent with two schoolgirl friends, when we were all sixteen, 'table tapping'. For the uninitiated, this means three or more people sitting around a three-legged wooden table, hands on the table with thumbs and little fingers joined to make a circle, and asking questions to which the table would reply by tapping on the floor with one leg – two taps for yes and one for no. I still do not know how this worked, but am prepared to swear that none of us present was responsible. The table creaked and seemed to come alive, and the taps followed. It all had to be done in the dark and was rather frightening. We asked several questions and received confusing replies, and then we asked it to tap out in tens the age of our headmistress at school (a dreary old spinster with a sharp nose for ferreting out misdemeanors, and no sense of humour). The table tapped out one hundred and fifty. We didn't think this could be true, somehow, and then one of my friends whose sense of humour was decidedly quirky, asked it to tap out in tens the age at which I was going to die. I let it get up to seventy, and then broke the chain in my panic.

Such was my sole experience in dabbling with the occult, when I met Beth and Ida Perry – practising spiritualists. They were both Waafs on the staff at Group, and when I tentatively expressed an interest in spiritualism, they fastened onto me like leeches. I think they sensed in me a possible convert to their beliefs, merely because I was curious, or perhaps they genuinely liked me – I don't know. I couldn't help noticing that they spent all their off-duty time racing down to London to what they called 'a sitting', which turned out to be another name for a seance. They invited me to take part in the next one and I went along with them, having no idea what I was getting in to.

One of their friends was a medium, and once a month those of their group who could get there would assemble at her flat in south London for a seance. I was given to understand it was an honour for me to have been invited, and I was very much on trial. I went there quite ready to be impressed but came away merely bewildered. All the others thought it was so wonderful and I couldn't understand what I was missing.

When we arrived I was introduced to the medium, Helen, a quite ordinary, sandy-haired woman in her mid-thirties, and the rest of the group, Dora and Leo and Katy and Humphrey, and everyone made a great fuss of me. They raved about what they called my 'Van Gogh' hair (a naturally pale yellow at the time), and Helen welcomed me because, as she said, I had fairies sitting on my shoulder. I instinctively had a quick look but I couldn't see a damned thing. Oh dear! It does sound silly at this distance of time, but then, green as grass, I lapped it all up. I'd never met people like this before and really did not know what to make of them.

The sitting began. We all sat in dead silence waiting for Helen to get the urge, but for about ten minutes nothing happened, just heavy breathing all round. Then suddenly she got up and made for the piano. She crashed out a few chords and started to talk to us in a different voice through her 'control', who was (of course), a Red Indian – White Cloud or Black Feet or something like that. The nature of this talk rather surprised me. It seemed that each member of the group had a question to ask concerning his or her own life, and the whole thing turned out to be a kind of Agony Aunt column – you took along your problem and were advised what you should do, and you did it. You didn't argue with White Feet or Red Cloud because he knew best. It all seemed to me one more way of getting people to stop thinking for themselves – a highly convenient and complacent way of life – for if you took the advice offered and made a mess of things, then it could always be someone else's fault.

After about an hour and a half the meeting broke up. I made no contribution to the evening, but Helen said I now had fairies sitting on *both* shoulders. People came up to me with glowing faces and said, Wasn't it wonderful? I didn't want to hurt their feelings, having been brought up to be polite, so I tried to look happy and muttered something about Helen playing the piano very well.

I never really became part of the group. I was the awkward one who kept asking difficult questions, such as, Why isn't Leo in the Forces? and What war work do Helen and Dora do? Besides, none of them had any sense of humour and I ruined many a high-flown discussion by making jokes. Then when, a few months later, I met the man who was to become my husband, I was told in no uncertain terms that Helen – wouldn't you know it? – did not approve. He was not 'the one' and I was expected to drop him forthwith. Naturally this was like a red rag to a bull and I refused to even consider such a course of action. My actual words I believe were something in the line of telling Helen to mind her own business and to keep her nose out of my affairs, but Beth and Ida could never understand why I reacted so violently. I had a deep-seated feeling that the whole business of seances, trying to get in touch with spirits and souls who had 'passed on' was wrong and dangerous for me, and I did not want to get involved. Even if it wasn't dangerous, it was certainly silly and I could think of better things to do with my time.

Gradually I drifted apart from Beth and Ida, but I am always grateful to them because they also introduced me to the other great interest in their lives – ballet.

Pinned above Beth's bed, next to the card proclaiming her to be a spiritualist, was a photograph of a male dancer from the newly formed Royal Ballet, and I came in one day soon after I arrived at Huntingdon to find a knot of giggling girls peering up at this dancer, who was poised on one foot, wearing an agonised expression and very *tight* tights. No marks for guessing which portion of his anatomy all their eyes were rivetted to. They had never seen anything like it before – only statues of course, with a well-placed fig leaf, but that wan't the same thing. This chap was real, performing in public, for Heaven's sake!

Before long, I was introduced to the hysterical world of balletomania and had had several overnight trips to Sadlers Wells theatre to queue up for the cheap seats, once even queueing all night. It was all so different from the Air Force – that was one of the attractions. But, hysteria apart, these trips opened my eyes to a new world of music and beauty, of which there hadn't, of necessity, been a great deal during the last six years. I became one of the enthusiastic mob (mostly female) who hung over the balcony rail at the end of performances of *Swan Lake* and *Coppelia*, yelling for Margot and Bobby (Fonteyn and Helpmann), as if we knew them personally. And then racing back to Huntingdon to plot a few more charts, sometimes hitch-hiking all the way to save the fare money. It was all marvellous therapy after the years of strain and hard work.

The only other event at Huntingdon that I recall with any clarity was when I had my first ever flight in an aircraft – and for a time I was quite determined that it was going to be my last.

After the cessation of hostilities, there were hundreds of aircrew cooling their heels in airfields up and down the country with nothing much to do. No more German targets to bomb, nothing to do except circuits and bumps, navigation trips and map reading. The demob was as slow for them as it was for us. I suppose it makes sense – it was no use flooding the post-war employment market with too many job-hunting men all at once, but we all had a terrible feeling of anti-climax. Six years of war were over and most of us were barely out of school when it began, so what came next? Something had to be found for the men to do with their time, so someone had the bright idea of introducing 'Cook's Tours' – trips over France and Germany in a Lancaster for any of the non-flying staff who cared to take advantage of it, including Waafs. At least it might help to mitigate the boredom. I put my name on the list with everyone else, but was absolutely dumbfounded when I was told one day that it had come up, along with that of one of the other Waafs, and if we wanted to go we were to report to RAF Wyton at 10.00 hours the next day.

The other Waaf was the aforementioned Olive, who had a face like an uncooked currant bun, even to the little black eyes. I must state that she was not my favourite person. She was a sly one, a crawler, with a facade of laughing bonhomie which I was convinced was egg-shell thin. One of her least charming habits involved our night duties in the Met Office. At that time, although the night work had to continue, we were not very busy, and instead of having two Waafs on all night we were allowed to split the night between us, changing over at 2am. Olive, when she was sharing the night with me, had the habit of coming up to me about 7.30pm and saying in a sympathetic voice, 'You *do* look tired! Why don't I do the first half and you have an early night, and I'll wake you at two o'clock?', knowing full well how awful it is to be woken out of a deep sleep at 2am to start work. I must have been awfully slow, I *never* got in ahead of her and was always the poor mutt who staggered into the office in the small hours, bleary-eyed and half-dead, while Olive, yawning profusely and clutching her hot water bottle to her bosom, was able to trip down the path to her waiting bed and not surface till about midday the next day.

And here I was, booked to fly over Germany with her. I had a fleeting thought of what fun it would have been to do this trip with Rosemary. But there it was, the chance of a lifetime, and although I was petrified with fright, I couldn't turn it down. We were taken the few miles out to Wyton by RAF transport and in a short time, smiling falsely at each other and with our cumbersome parachutes bumping round our legs, we found ourselves walking out to the plane for our first flight.

To the crew it was a routine trip and one they had made many times before by night. We were scheduled to fly out over East Anglia and the North Sea, crossing the coast of Holland and then on to the Ruhr as far as Cologne, returning over the same route. It was a beautiful day with small cumulus clouds and about thirty miles visibility, and it should have been a great experience, but unfortunately I felt deadly sick all the way and could hardly bear to look out. The aircraft had a peculiar motion, rather like a small boat in a heavy ocean swell, or rather what I imagined that must feel like, never having been out on the open sea in a small boat. I wondered how these men had managed to endure thirty or more trips in what must have been far worse conditions than this; in bad weather, being shot at, having to concentrate on map reading and peering through bomb sites, and watching out all the time for enemy fighters. Perhaps they were too busy to feel queasy, but as far as I was concerned, before we had been airborne half an hour I felt like crying out, 'Stop the plane, I want to get off!' Not a chance of course – I was stuck there in my seat for the next five or six hours. I was in the middle of the aircraft next to the wireless operator, who read a book the whole way and ignored me completely. This was just as well, because I must have looked pea green, and it didn't make me feel any better to watch Olive sitting up front chatting to the pilot and navigator, obviously having the time of her life.

When we were flying over Holland I did steel myself to look out and I remember seeing where miles of land had been submerged under sea water to keep the Germans out, and houses, trees and roads were still under water. Those poor Dutch people, it must have been awful having the Germans right on their border and no English Channel to keep them out. And now they had the immense task of reclaiming all this land and rebuilding all their homes.

As we approached the Ruhr, scene of so many destructive raids by the RAF and the American Air Force, and so much loss of life, there seemed to be nothing but ruins in every direction. The wireless operator roused himself to point out to me a circle of pale pink rubble – literally not one brick left upon another – which was the town of Wesel. What did they all think now, I wondered, all those German people living down there in the wreckage of their homes, remembering how their Fuhrer had promised them that not one bomb would fall upon the Fatherland? I've never been to Germany since, never seen anymore of it than I saw from the air that day in 1945, and I can't say I've ever wanted to.

At Cologne we turned for home, circling the great cathedral at what felt like an angle of forty five degrees. The massive stone structure stood out bravely amidst the miles of destruction, and the crew became interested as they hadn't seen it in daylight before. It had certainly been built to last, and although we could see it had lost a lot of windows and the stonework was damaged, it was obviously going to be standing there a few more years yet. As for me, once we had turned right round and were headed west again, I began to feel my worries were nearly over.

Wrong again. We hadn't gone very far when we met up with another Lancaster returning from a Cook's Tour, and to my horror the two aircraft then flew wing-tip to wing-tip all the way home. Sometimes we were a few feet higher, sometimes the other one was. I was sitting there as tense as a coiled up spring, waiting for the wings to touch and all of us to hurtle to the ground in a ball of fire. No-one else in our aircraft appeared to be the least bit concerned, but my relief as we finally drew near the coast of England again and then began our descent to the safety of solid earth was so great that I made a little promise to myself that I would never again set foot in an aeroplane, so long as I could be permitted to survive this one trip.

But all the same, it was fun to telephone home from Huntingdon that evening and electrify the family by saying, 'You'll never guess where I've just been!' and listen to their admiring and incredulous comments.

Gradually, as the demobilisation began to take effect, the smaller satellite airfields were closed down and the surplus staff posted mainly to permanent stations. One day the news broke that 8 Group was to be disbanded and our office would be closing.

By that time Tommy had left us and the Chief Met Officer was a man called Mr Donaldson. After Tommy any change was bound to be for the worse, but really! He was a tall, thin man of about fifty and he looked like a bloodhound, even to the wet nose, and had a nauseating habit of drooling sentimentally about his wife to anyone who would listen. We, with the arrogance of extreme youth, thought this was disgusting at his age. With his long miserable face and long red nose which he was perpetually wiping, and his habit of comparing each one of us with his paragon of a wife, we hated him. And he hated us. When the time came to close the office, he took great pleasure in posting us all as far away from our homes as he possibly could.

I found I was being sent to some ghastly hole, miles from civilisation, on top of the Lincolnshire wolds, and as I trekked sullenly north, little did I know how the course of my life was about to be permanently changed.

9

Romance – Air Force style

I had thought that the one good thing about being posted to a permanent, that is a pre-war, RAF Station, was that at least the Waaf quarters should consist of solid, brick-built barracks and not the Nissen huts which had been my home so far. I had forgotten that before the war there had been no Women's Auxiliary Air Force to build barrack blocks for, as the Force only came into being in 1939.

The journey by train from Cambridge to Lincoln was tedious, involving several changes, and on arrival I was met by the usual RAF truck for the half hour's run into Binbrook village and from there up the steep hill to the RAF Station on its plateau above the low lying plains. When the truck had dumped me and my kit-bag at the Guard Room and I had a chance to look around me, I spied in the middle distance a cluster of substantial looking buildings. This was hopeful, and the Guard Room Corporal confirmed that that was where I would find the Met Office. But when I enquired about the location of the Waaf Site, I was told to climb back on the wagon. Ten minutes later, at the end of a long downward-sloping track, the Waafery appeared out of the mist, the usual huddle of rounded Nissen huts, surrounded by the usual mud. My already depressed spirits sank a few notches lower.

I hadn't been in a very good mood when I started out on this journey. A few days previously I had paid a quick visit to Bourn, which had not yet closed down, to say goodbye to those of my acquaintances who were still there, and to find out what had happened to Rosemary. She hadn't written to me for several weeks and I was beginning to wonder what stage her marriage plans had arrived at, but wasn't at all prepared for the news that greeted me.

'Married!', said Mary in disgust, 'Two weeks ago, and never invited any of us!'

'We thought she might have told you,' added Nancy. 'You were her friend.'

Well, some friend. Apparently Hank's divorce had come through sooner than expected, the deed was done one Saturday afternoon in the local Registrar's Office, and she came back to Bourn wearing a wedding ring like a brass curtain ring (Mary's words), to await her discharge from the Waaf.

I didn't see her while I was at Bourn, which I was not sorry about. I was inclined to echo Mary's disgust. It didn't seem to me the way to behave towards someone with whom you had shared a good many midnight hours, swopping confidences and generally letting your hair down, not to mention the many other evenings when we had had such fun with Henry and Jimmy, and I felt rather aggrieved at being treated this way. It certainly seemed that a chapter of my life was closing, and I felt even more disgruntled when I found out that the other girls had all managed to get postings near their homes for their final few months in the Service. I was the only one who was moving further away, and that knowledge didn't improve my outlook on things in general.

By the time I had started unpacking once more in one more Nissen hut, I was feeling really low. What I had so far seen of Binbrook held no charms for me – it was bare, isolated, and I didn't really want to seek out yet another Met Office with another set of people to get to know, now that the war was over, and there was no reason that I could see for us to continue plotting charts and reading instruments. As I read in someone else's book, the trouble with the end of the war was just that – the end of the war. The bite had gone out of everything; it all seemed to be a frightful drag. On top of which, I think Binbrook must have been the coldest RAF Station in England. Situated on top of its hill in the middle of Lincolnshire, it took the full blast of the east wind all the way from Russia – nothing to stop it, you see. There wasn't another hill between Binbrook and the Urals, and when there was a wind on (most of the time), you could lean on it. On the few occasions when the wind was not blowing a gale, the fog descended like a shroud. I can count on the fingers of one hand the days when the weather was pleasant during my ten months there. One day in May I remember, the sun shone, the wind dropped and larks flew straight up from the fields, singing with astonishment when they felt the warmth in the air. But most of the time it was plain awful. Whenever we cycled to work, or indeed from work, we met the full force of that malevolent wind. Talk about blowing the cobwebs away!

Once I had got myself unpacked, it was 5pm and the day shift girls from the various departments were coming off-duty, including two of the Met girls, Jean and Marjorie. They were both Londoners so this cheered me up no end, and we were soon making our way to the Mess for supper and then up to the office for me to meet some of the others. Here, I discovered the Met Office boasted a Waaf sergeant, a corporal, and seven LACWs like myself. It's not that Binbrook was such an important station to warrant all this staff, but as the size of the RAF contracted more and more, Waafs were posted there from the closing satellite stations and at one point there were twelve of us. Now we couldn't complain of overwork. Mostly we complained of boredom. We were all marking time, waiting for our demob, and tended to look back wistfully at what was past and familiar, rather than forward to the unknown future.

There were two Waaf Officers, General Duties, on the strength at Binbrook, and they were a bit of a trial to us. Perhaps they were bored too, but whatever the reason the Met girls were always in trouble for one reason or another. Mostly it was that good old chestnut – missing morning parade. Our usual excuse, that we were on duty, didn't wash so well now, there being so many of us around. It was suggested that surely we could spare one, or even two, to put in a token appearance now and then? Well, no, not really Ma'am, there were still charts to plot, and observations to send to Group, and instruments to read – and the unspoken implication, ever present, was that we were Grade 2 technicians, and if she wanted to make up the numbers on parade surely she could find a few more pen-pushers in nine-to-five jobs? There was no doubt about it, we were not popular with those above us. We didn't have 'team spirit' any more, (Miss Brodie would have been proud of us!).

We knew all the aircrews and were on Christian name terms with most of them. Binbrook was free and easy. It had an Australian squadron when I first went there and the Aussies do not stand on ceremony. A lot of the best-looking Waafs on the station had acquired Australian boyfriends, and two of the Met girls had recently married them and were impatiently waiting to get on the ship for Aussie-land to join their husbands. Their minds were obviously not on meteorological work, and as the squadron gradually decreased in numbers with each little batch that left for home, farewell parties were a regular occurrence in the office and I began to think that perhaps Binbrook was not such a bad place after all. All this jollity, however, did not go down well with our two female gauleiters.

The one major event which happened to me at Binbrook, and which was going to change my life, was that I met the man I was eventually to marry, although a lot of water would flow under the bridge before the wedding took place.

I met him at a dance held in the Airmen's Mess (so romantic!), when I'd only been at Binbrook three weeks. I'd been on duty in the Met Office since 8am, and managed to comb my hair and put on some lipstick before going straight down to the dance with June, one of the other Met Waafs. I was not, for once, wearing my battledress trousers, but had put on my uniform skirt with my battledress top. This was the most flattering get-up that we had, so therefore it was banned. The battledress trousers were inclined to go baggy and the uniform jacket was a bit severe, so whenever we could get away with it we wore the other two items, and tended to let our hair float over our collars – also banned.

I was just beginning to enjoy myself at this dance, when up came Section Officer Hutchcroft, the junior Waaf Officer, the light of battle in her eyes.

'Airwoman,' she said, frostily. 'You are improperly dressed. Please leave at once, or get changed. And pin your hair up!'

This hair rule was one I was always breaking, unintentionally. It is very difficult to keep your hair up off your collar if you are afflicted with a short neck. What with my hair, and my collar and tie, and my hat, and a short neck somewhere in the middle, unless I had a two-inch all-over bubble cut it was well nigh impossible to prevent hair and collar overlapping.

I couldn't argue with her, knowing I was in the wrong, so in a thoroughly bad mood I free-wheeled down the hill to the Waafery, determined to go straight to bed and to Hell with the dance. But Fate took a hand, as it has a habit of doing, and the first person I encountered in the hut was Barbara, who was putting the final touches to her make-up before going to the dance herself. She was delighted to see me, as it meant she would not have to go on her own, and she stood over me while, complaining bitterly, I changed into my jacket and returned with her to the revels. And the first person I danced with was 'him'.

I can't remember now what my first impressions were. It's all a long time ago and I've been married to him for thirty-nine years. But I wasn't struck by any thunder-bolts or lightning flashes, and when talking about the dance afterwards in the Met Office I merely remarked to the officer on duty that I'd met a very nice corporal and he'd asked me to go to the Station cinema with him on Saturday. From little acorns grow mighty oaks – or something like that. The immediate outcome was that I now had someone to take me around, and I used to brag a bit about 'my' Corporal.

He was a Corporal Fitter/Armourer, but had started his RAF career as a trainee pilot with a lot of other young hopefuls. This was in 1941, when the Battle of Britain was over and thousands of young men were flocking into the RAF, hoping to become Fighter Pilots, or failing that one of the slightly less glamorous Bomber boys. I think at the time the RAF had more volunteers than it could cope with and much weeding out was done, but in his case he blotted his copybook good and proper by doing a bit of unauthorised low flying over a south Devonshire town, frightening all the old ladies. So he was suspended, removed from flying and directed into another trade. He did an eight month fitter/armourer course ending up his training with top marks and a corporal's stripes, and then did several months' instructing before being sent to a ground crew on a Bomber Command airfield. With hindsight, it was probably the best thing that could have happened to him, otherwise he would no doubt have ended up as a Bomber Pilot, and no-one knows better than I what a dead-end occupation *that* was. But I don't suppose he saw it that way at the time.

Having now met each other, it seemed that everywhere I went on camp I would come face to face with him, usually with his entourage of armourers fanning out behind him. He was taller than most of them, his nickname being 'Lofty', and always looked a lot cleaner than his oil-stained gang. The armourers were the scruffiest erks to be seen anywhere – untidy, good-natured, mostly wearing leather jerkins over their battle dress (held together with pieces of wire), and mostly in need of a shave as well. They were quite intimidating to a poor Waaf struggling along in the teeth of a gale, on a bike in a skirt. Not only that, but once it was established that their corporal had an interest in me, every movement I made, almost every breath I drew, was reported back to him, including a very innocent ride I had one evening round the perimeter track in a jeep driven by one of the Flying Control Officers. One of the armourers was known as Spike, and he petrified me. He was the largest and hairiest and pimpliest and dirtiest of them all, not at all the sort of person you would wish to meet up an alley on a dark night. But in fact he was a big softy, and I believe was quite hurt because I was scared of him.

When things were at this interesting stage, to my irritation the senior of the two Waaf officers who were the bane of our lives developed an interest in 'my' Corporal. I don't know if this was especially unusual, or maybe even against King's Regulations (so many things were), but Flight Officer Gregory was forever pursuing him with offers of theatre tickets and weekends in London. As far as I know he never took her up on any of these, and that may have been the reason why I was her least favourite Waaf on the station. I was always running up against her and being told that I had a shoelace undone, or my buttons needed polishing, or my hair was touching my collar, Airwoman! She certainly had a grudge against me. She would appear at the gates of the Waaf Site about 10.45pm, armed with a torch half the size of the Flamborough lighthouse, when upwards of a dozen couples would be propping up the fence saying goodnight. The torch would be shone on all of us in turn, but mostly me, with the terse comment, 'It's time you were in bed, Airwoman!'

Well! We could all have thought of suitable answers to that one, but the rigid framework in which we lived dictated that we button up our lips, bite our tongues and suffer in silence. This aspect of the military life was what really got to us, being told what to do by our so-called superiors. Now that our *raison d'etre*, helping to win a war, had been removed, we were all counting the days to our release and petty regulations, necessary though they might be, were becoming very irksome.

At any rate, Miss Gregory and I always eyed each other with open hostility. She had the edge on me from the point of view of rank, but I felt secure in the knowledge that 'J' (my Corporal) didn't want to take her out anyway.

Later on, she was posted. I didn't at the time know where to, but when I had only about two months to go I too was posted, to Scampton near Lincoln, and who was the first person I saw when I booked into the Waaf Guard Room? Flt Off Gregory seated behind the desk. 'Good afternoon, Huckle,' she greeted me, a look of malicious glee on her face. 'Welcome to Scampton!' All I could manage in return was a sickly smile and a feeble, 'Thank you, Ma'am.' Luckily, in a place the size of Scampton it was easy enough to keep out of her path, and this I did quite successfully until my turn came for demobilisation.

One of the few places we could go to on the camp at Binbrook without risk of being observed by the hierarchy was the Station cinema. If I remember correctly, officers sat in the front few rows and NCOs and other lower forms of life had the rest. Our problem, J. and I, was that wherever we sat we did tend to have a row of armourers planted behind us, and instead of watching the screen their eyes would be fixed on us to see what we were getting up to. But there was no malice in their interest and I sometimes had the feeling that they were waiting for me to turn round and hand them a bag of toffees, with instructions to share them out fairly and not throw the papers on the floor.

By the end of 1945, those of us left in the Forces were all, I think, getting a bit tired of the sameness and predictability of the food which was dished out to us. Eggs were always in short supply and I suppose the reason was that during the war we were not getting our usual supply from Denmark and the Low Countries, owing to the German occupation. I mean, surely the English hens were laying at the same rate as they did in peacetime? In the RAF eggs were mostly reserved for the air crew's after-ops breakfasts and this we fully understood. It was right and proper and as it should be. But there didn't seem to be any more around after the war was over. There were sometimes, but rarely, eggs for breakfast in the Airmens' Mess, but these were eggs-as-they-came, and they usually came fried and cold and congealed on a plate on a Sunday morning. So imagine our joy when we discovered 'Eggy'.

We never discovered her real name, but she ran a small cafe down in the village and she appeared to have an inexhaustible supply of eggs. Of an evening, Eggy's was a popular rendezvous for those of us off-duty. We would brave the icy blast, stagger down the hill and stuff ourselves to the gills with scrambled or poached eggs on buttery toast, or light-as-air omelettes, followed by giant sized mugs of good, strong tea and thick slices of bread and farm butter, all priced to suit the hard-up airman's pocket. It was a feast fit for a king, and afterwards when we left we felt well fortified to tackle the hill back up to camp. Once J. called her Eggy to her face, and then had to quickly explain that this was a term of admiration, not derision. I fear she was not amused.

Every so often, some minor disaster would occur on the Waaf site and we would all have to suffer the consequences because the perpetrator would never own up. It was usually something quite silly and trivial, like leaving the taps running in the bath huts or over-stuffing the dustbins so that mess and litter was spread all over the ground, but sometimes someone's carelessness resulted in the whole inadequate drainage system being completely overloaded and clogged up. Then some of the RAF ground staff were called in to dig holes all over the place, and we girls were most unpopular. This happened once while I was at Binbrook, and we were all jailed for a week – well, confined to our quarters, really, but it amounted to the same thing. We were only allowed off the site to go to work, and this is where we shift girls scored as we worked round the clock and had to leave the camp after dark when all the day workers had to stay indoors. But it was a great nuisance, anyway, and we did not suffer in silence.

It was October when I arrived at Binbrook, and as winter approached the air became bitingly cold. I was always cold at Binbrook. All the men on the camp were housed in brick built barrack blocks, and J. even had a little room to himself with a *radiator*. (Or so he told me. Naturally, Waafs were never allowed inside the sacred portals of the men's living quarters.) This knowledge made our spartan quarters even harder to bear. The only heating in the Waaf huts was from the temperamental iron stove in the centre of each hut, and anyone who has had to struggle with one of these objects will appreciate what I'm talking about. We only had such wood as we could scrounge, and to light a fire with the bare minimum of paper and wood, plus uncooperative coke is difficult to say the least. The coke just doesn't want to burn. We had to take it in turns day by day to get this monstrosity going, or freeze to death, and the hours I've spent wasting matches, holding sheets of paper against the opening to create an up-draught, blowing like a whale whenever a tiny spark appeared! Mind, once it did get going it would then do its best to roast us alive, and the girls with beds nearest to it had to move back to escape the heat. But for the most part we shivered in our beds that winter, heaping on more and more blankets, which seemed to be made of a mixture of cardboard and lead and only increased the weight without increasing the heat.

Finally, J. got tired of my everlasting complaints, took pity on me and made me a small electric fire. He bought an electric ring from Woolworths and scrounged the pieces of metal to make the stand. (He was a scrounger *par excellence*.) Against this we could warm our tiny frozen hands and boil a kettle to fill our hot water bottles. Rather apprehensively I let the other girls use it, on the strict understanding that when they had finished with it they unplugged it and stowed it away somewhere out of sight of our two gauleiters, hopefully after it had cooled down a bit. But of course I was always coming off-duty to find the thing burning away merrily in an empty hut. My guardian angel must have been working overtime as the hut never actually caught fire, and as far as I am aware neither of our overseers suspected that we were harbouring such a forbidden utensil in the Met Waafs' hut.

For me it was certainly a healthy life, living up on the wolds after two years in the marshy lowlands of Cambridgeshire and Huntingdon. Pedalling up to the office in the mornings, with the bike wheels crunching on the thick white frost, I would arrive with bright red cheeks and breath coming out like steam, and once the Met Officer commented, after I had given him a cheerful, early morning smile, 'You don't know what a difference it makes to your face when you smile! You should do it more often.'

This gave me pause, and when I returned to the hut I tried out a few grins into a hand mirror, and decided he was quite right! Henceforth I went around grinning like an idiot, which wasn't difficult. I was feeling much happier than I had for two years. Things seemed to be going my way at last. The war was over, I had a steady boyfriend who wasn't likely to be shot down over the Ruhr, and I was working with a bunch of very congenial people. The other Met girls, Sheila, Marjorie, Babs, Dora and Jean were all very easy to get on with, and the Met Office was custom built for the job, with benches that were properly lit and stools the right height for us to work from. We had a rain gauge and an anemometer for wind speeds – no more guess work with the wet finger held aloft – and, Thank God, no more slippery ladders to the roof. The instruments were housed in a screen which was approached by a paved path, and now that blackout restrictions were lifted we could use outside electric light. It was all quite civilised and there were so many of us girls there that we could take it in turn to do the observations. And, wonder of wonders, soon after I arrived word came from Group that there was no longer any need to do hourly observations at night. We could actually sleep on the camp bed between the midnight and 6am observations. This was sheer luxury after years of stumbling out into the dark at all hours, forcing our eyes to stay open, and yawning fit to split our faces in two. The difficulty now as far as I was concerned was not being able to stay awake all night, but being able to sleep all night. I kept on waking up in a panic, thinking I had missed an observation, and it took quite some while to get my internal clock re-adjusted to normal waking and sleeping hours.

The other Met personnel, apart from the Waafs, have remained rather a blur in my mind, with the exception of an obnoxious little civilian type known as Thursby. One assumes he also had a Christian name and that his mother loved him, but one thing is certain, nobody else at Binbrook did. He was young and madly enthusiastic for all things meteorological, with the exception of the teleprinter which he was always messing up, getting the paper stuck and so on, and leaving us to sort it out when we came on duty. Behind his thick spectacles, his eyes positively blazed at the sight of a completed chart just waiting to have lines drawn on it, and he was always very quick off the mark with his instant weather forecasts whenever any aircrews were planning a jaunt somewhere. He was nearly always right, too, so very seldom did anyone get the chance of really taking him down a peg or two. I think we despised him in our high-handed way because as he had joined the Met service after the end of the war, he had never actually been in uniform. He *would* insist on checking our observations before we sent them to Group on the teleprinter, and this we regarded as a deadly insult, most of us having been doing them unchecked for over three years. He also looked over our shoulders while we plotted the charts, watching for any slip-ups. Thursby thought he knew it all.

Often, when I was cycling through the camp after coming off duty, I would spy Thursby in the distance beavering along, head down against the gale, full of eagerness to get back on the job and spot any mistakes we had made during his absence. There was only one thing to do in these circumstances – make a quick, right-angled turn down the next convenient track. Once I did this without looking where I was going and went straight into the backs of nine armourers who were ambling towards the Mess for supper, and had to be disentangled from my machine, picked up and dusted off, which they did with all the gleeful enthusiasm which Thursby reserved for drawing his heavy black frontal lines on our neatly drawn charts.

One of my friends at Binbrook was Sheila – tall, awkward, difficult, but a very bright girl. When I wasn't rushing out to meet J. somewhere, I was usually chatting with Sheila. She was planning to get into university on demobilisation, to study history, and wherever she was posted she was accompanied by a large wooden crate of study books. She must have had a posting, or else obtained her demob while I was still at Binbrook, because I have a distinct memory of Sheila hammering nails into this crate before despatching it to her new destination, and scornfully refusing all help from J., who was standing by with the hammer and nails. She could knock a nail in as well as any man, she said, and at once proceeded to do so. She could discourse at great length on the history of Europe, illustrating how little I knew on this vast subject (having ducked out of history lessons at the age of thirteen). The subject had bored me witless at school, but on Sheila's lips it all came alive, and forced me to the conclusion that it wasn't history which was boring, but those who tried to teach it.

She also played the flute. The unusual thing about this was that at Binbrook there was an engineering type called Matthew, a corporal, who also played this instrument, and it didn't take long for the two to discover each other. Very often in the evening one could hear mysterious melodies issuing from some hidden corner of a hangar or a deserted office – Sheila and Matthew having a flute practice. This was regarded and listened to with some incredulity by the majority of the airmen, whose main ambition regarding Waafs had much to do with getting them into dark corners, like behind the Naafi, and nothing whatever to do with playing the flute or any other instrument. They were a couple of originals, Sheila and Matthew. She finally made it to university, after which to my regret I lost touch with her.

J. and I spent that Christmas at our separate homes, but were back on camp for the New Year celebrations, the first new year of peacetime for seven years, and as 1945 drew to a close most of us were beginning to look tentatively ahead to the future when we would no longer be bound by the rules and regulations which had fenced us in for so long, and to wonder where we would all be in another twelve months.

10

Full circle

It was a winter not of discontent but of change and new ideas – a change of direction for me and a widening of horizons.

I knew that when at last I was demobilised from the Waaf I would have to return to my peacetime occupation as a secretary in London, for the simple reason that my employers had been paying me my full salary all the time I had been in the Forces, that is, making up the difference between my Waaf pay and what I would have been earning with them. I suppose it was one way of ensuring that staff returned to the fold, but I'm not so sure that it was a good idea as far as the staff was concerned. It pinned us down and made us feel that we couldn't *not* go back without feeling terribly guilty. Because of this arrangement, while I was in the Waaf I always had plenty of spending money, but there weren't a whole lot of things to spend it on. I wasn't saving up to get married, I wasn't very interested in jewellery, and clothes, which I could have been interested in, came under the category of things to look at in shop windows but not to buy, because of the very limited amount of clothing coupons one was allowed to have. I can't remember now whether in fact we were allowed any at all while we were in the Waaf, but I know that for the few years after I became a civilian again and clothes rationing still went on, the ration allocation was so small that the prospect of buying, for instance, a new winter coat was exceedingly small for most women, especially those with children, whose needs had to come first.

Even knitting wool was on ration, but for a time a keen knitter could go into a shop and buy up hanks of thin darning wool (un-rationed) and use that to knit with, until some spoilsport in the Government ruined that idea by decreeing that all darning wool should be cut into approximately twenty inch lengths before it was put into the shops. Even so, I did meet one girl at Binbrook who had knitted a whole twin set from darning wool cut into short lengths, *weaving all the ends together* as she knitted! – and she showed me the finished product to prove it. It looked terrible.

But for me everything was now gradually working out, slowly. Although I could see marriage appearing in the distance, it was still a long way off. The war had interrupted and postponed many a career, J's amongst them, and he had three years' university ahead of him before he would be in any position to marry. Those late 1940s now seem light years away from the customs prevailing in present day society. You did not go off and set up house with the man in your life and perhaps think about marriage if it seemed like a good idea, after a year or two. It was not done. You became decently engaged and made plans to get married six months or a year ahead, and in the meantime you lived decorously at home with your parents. The permissive society of the 60's and 70's was not yet dreamed of.

So, back to the typing I knew I would go, but at least now I could see an end to it.

Meantime, I really enjoyed that winter of 1945/6, in

spite of the disgusting weather. The strain of possible air raids and bad news from abroad was at last removed from our lives, and being still in the Air Force, and single, my only responsibilities were to do my job properly and polish my buttons at regular intervals. I went to every Station dance and was always sure of having a partner – either J. or one of his pals. Sometimes he was roped in to be the MC at these dances, which, for those who know only disco dancing, means Master of Ceremonies, and it was he who announced that the next dance would be a waltz, or a foxtrot, and was not supposed to dance himself until everyone else was on the floor. J. was a good dancer having been to dancing classes as a small boy, and enjoyed them, in contrast to his younger brother who dug his heels in and absolutely refused to do anything so sissy.

He really had himself very well organised at Binbrook. For instance, on cinema nights we were always assured of good seats as one of his armourers was regularly on the door collecting tickets, and he made sure we had a good view. I came off well in the area of sweet coupons, too. Rationing of sweets, like food and clothing, was continued for several years after the war was over, and people like me with a sweet tooth used to bemoan the meagre ration of sweets and chocolate we were allowed. However, as I didn't smoke I used to hand over my cigarette coupons, and received the equivalent in sweet coupons from J's legion of armourers. I don't know what sort of a pistol he held to their heads, but I personally was quite happy and had never been looked after so well in my life. J. decided he wanted a photograph of me, and although I did tease him a bit about this – what did he want a photograph of me for when I was there in front of him most of the time? – at his insistence I finally went and had it done. The photographic section on the camp was not very busy, having no aerial photos of enemy territory to decipher any more, and one of the photographic LACs got himself onto a good thing by setting himself up taking portraits, mostly of Waafs but a few airmen too. As films for private cameras were in very short supply – what wasn't? – I went along to him to be recorded for posterity, although being gloomily aware that I didn't photograph very well.

However, the result seemed to please J. and even I thought it was passable. The photographer had obviously been studying portraits of Betty Grable and other film stars and was trying to be very artistic, with much back lighting and fluffing out of hair, and I must admit that my hair (touching my shoulders, naturally), did look nice. I kept 'the smile' rigidly fixed and hoped that a very untimely spot on my chin would not be too obvious.

All sorts of schemes were thought up to keep people busy and occupied during the trying period of 'waiting to be demobbed.' Evening courses were arranged on all sorts of subjects, which we as shift workers were unfortunately not able to take advantage of fully, as we had to work during the evenings. J. went off to another station at one point for a two week course on shoe repairing and general leatherwork – not that he was thinking of setting up in business as a cobbler, but figuring that a free training on any practical skill was worth having. Needless to say, he took my photograph with him.

I kept my fingers crossed figuratively during the first few months of our acquaintance that neither of us would be sent elsewhere on a permanent posting – permanent until demob, that is – because I had seen quite a few promising romances nipped in the bud by one or the other partner being whipped away by the unfeeling powers-that-be, and when a relationship is developing you do need a few weeks of togetherness to allow it to mature. We were lucky. When J. came back from his course, we simply carried on from where we had left off.

It still niggled me a bit that he could return to a centrally heated and solidly built barrack block, while the girls shivered in their huts. Sheila was in complete agreement with me on this subject, and the only disadvantage we could see to living in a barracks was having men in heavy boots walking about over your head. In the block where the RAF ground staff were housed, a similar problem did surface, not to do with boots but with Matthew's flute. The armourers all slept in a long room on the first floor, with J. in a small room to himself at the end, and it so happened that Matthew occupied the corresponding small room immediately underneath on the ground floor. This led to a certain amount of friction, as Matthew was in the habit of practising on his flute when he went to bed, and this was not appreciated by the men trying to sleep over his head, let alone those in the next room to him, and one day in the Mess they protested strongly and threatened to flatten him if this continued. Somewhat alarmed, he appealed over their heads to J., who promised to restrain his men if the provocation ceased forthwith. To the best of my knowledge peace reigned after that.

On the other hand, Matthew always knew what time J. came to bed at nights. They each had a radiator beside their beds, and very often when I was on night duty J. would return to bed very late (or should I say early?), after having been sitting with me in the Met Office, drinking coffee, chatting and so forth. He would flop wearily into bed, and clang! would go his iron bedstead against the radiator, and clang! would echo Matthew's radiator underneath, thus giving the game away. Then he would give J. a leer in the morning, 'Had another late night, have we?'

It amazes me when I think back, how we managed to go without sleep. At Bourn it was the custom to do three night duties in a row and then be off to Cambridge the next day without bothering to go to bed. Things were a bit easier at Binbrook in that direction as we could sleep between midnight and 6am, but I must admit that most nights I had considerably less sleep than that. J. didn't work nights and we had so much to talk about that it seemed a shame to waste precious time in sleep. We were still in the Air Force, postings could come out of the blue at any time, so every hour we could spend together was important.

One day I happened to mention that I didn't know one end of a bomb from the other, and wondered out loud what the bomb dump looked like. That was sufficient. At the next opportunity we were on our way to the Station Bomb Dump in the truck which J. had to get him around camp. The dump was of course strictly off-limits for all except armaments personnel, and I can't say it was very exciting when we got there. But for once the weather was fine, the place was right on the other side of the airfield on the edge of open country, so we wandered about a bit, picking wild flowers and so on, and on the way back in the truck who should we see approaching in the distance, on foot, but our old pal Flt Off Gregory. Up went an imperious hand and we had to stop. And what did we think we were doing?

'Just picking flowers, Ma'am,' J. replied mildly, and displayed the wilting daisies as proof. I, of course, was speechless.

She didn't say a word but her expression was enough, 'Pull the other one, its got bells on.' However, we were not actually doing anything unlawful when she saw us so there wasn't a thing she could do, I'm pleased to say. And, in any case, I think she realised she had met her match. J. was quite capable of staring her straight in the eye and swearing that black was white if it would get me out of a jam. I had found myself a champion! I'm not sure what authority, if any, Waaf Officers had over NCOs in the

RAF, but I'm pretty certain she wouldn't have got very far with him.

Another time, I had arranged to meet him in the Naafi, a popular meeting place on the camp, at 5pm. I arrived there at the due time and waited and waited, but no corporal appeared. After about an hour I gave up and retired to the Met Office, very much put out. Sometime later he did turn up, also very much put out but for a different reason. The squadron had been out on a practice bombing exercise and J. had been driving round the perimeter track that afternoon, inspecting the bomb bays of returned aircraft, and came back to park his vehicle in one of the empty hangars. This hangar was all closed up apart from one door, so he drove in in the semi-dark and reversed rapidly into what he thought was an empty corner without checking it first for parked vehicles. There was an appalling crash. Thoroughly alarmed he leapt out, and there behind the truck, rather squashed, was the remains of a private car belonging to one of the Station officers.

This was a disaster of some magnitude, and there was nothing for it but to seek the man out and tell him what had happened. 'I'm sorry sir, but I'm afraid I've scratched your car a bit!' Scratched it! There sat the poor thing with its windscreen smashed, its bonnet concertinered and the engine block on the front seat. What a sorry sight! It was a write-off. Never again would it scorch down the winding lanes to the Saracen's Head in Lincoln, the destination for most of the RAF Officers in the neighbourhood on their nights off, or even just down to the local in the village. In its heyday it must have been a good little vehicle, but now it was definitely finished.

The trouble was, it should never have been parked in that corner in the first place, so there wasn't much the owner could say, apart from making the air blue for half an hour or so. Eventually heads were put together, a suitable 'incident' was manufactured to satisfy all concerned, and the whole episode chalked up to experience, at least as far as J. was concerned. And a good lesson was learnt – always look before you reverse, especially when you are driving a 30 cwt. truck.

When the days grew longer in what passes for spring on that windy plateau, we used to go into Lincoln on our days off and have lunch in the Naafi Club. This was a superior kind of Naafi where NCOs and other ranks could have meals, and there were comfortable lounges to sit in and write letters or meet friends. And one couldn't say it wasn't needed. The officers had their Saracen's Head but the Lincoln Naafi Club really took some beating. We felt we were halfway back to civilian life, being off the camp and in the middle of an interesting town.

Lincoln rapidly became my second favourite town, largely because of its fabulous cathedral. My first sight of it, and to a slightly lesser extent every subsequent sighting, was breathtaking – no other word for it. It seemed to float above the town, particularly when one approached from the south, from the flats, and as you climbed Steep Hill and came nearer, so it became less of a mirage and more of a stone reality. We gazed, open-mouthed at the stately triple towers and the flying buttresses, then went inside and found the famous Lincoln Imp in the Angel Choir, and J. bought me a small silver imp for my charm bracelet. Afterwards we would walk around the Close and plan our future, and also talk about the war. The amazing thing to us was that we had both been in the Air Force for years, but hadn't met until the war was over. In fact our paths had not even come close until we both went to Binbrook.

J. had been with the now famous 617 Squadron for a time, and in talking about this he was able to furnish me with details of an incident which I had vaguely heard of while I was at Bourn.

Two or three months prior to the Dams Raid, when the new squadron was being formed in the spring of 1943, ground crew personnel from all over Bomber Command were selected and sent to Scampton, the best men at their respective jobs, for what they only knew at that time was going to be one special operation. J. was one of these in his capacity as fitter/ armourer, and he was there when an accident occurred which could have escalated into absolute disaster.

It was late afternoon on an operational day, and seventeen or eighteen Lancasters were marshalled on either side of the runway, all bombed-up and ready for take-off, when ops were suddenly cancelled. This did happen frequently for a variety of reasons, but it was usually because of a worsening of weather conditions either at home base or over the target area. I don't know what was the reason in this case, but in any event when ops were cancelled like this, late in the day when it was getting dark, for reasons of safety the armourers waited for daylight before de-bombing the aircraft. On this occasion, everything was shut down for the night but in the morning when the armourers were about to start work, something went wrong. I don't think anyone is sure what happened to cause it, but it is certain that one aircraft loaded with incendiaries started to burn and the fire spread to the two aircraft on either side. This was a highly dangerous situation. Emergency calls were immediately sent out, all air and ground personnel urgently tannoyed for, and fire engines went racing to the scene, but before the fires could be contained seven or eight aircraft were lost. It was absolute chaos. There were pilots getting their aircraft away on two engines, with armourers hanging on underneath checking the bombs, incendiaries blazing and HEs exploding in all directions.

J. was blown off his bicycle by the force of one explosion, while cycling from one aircraft to another, and woke up to find himself in hospital with concussion. There were incendiaries scattered all over the airfield for days, being picked up and made safe – another job for the armourers.

The episode was reported minimally in the Press, but played down like so much else during wartime. Not long afterwards the Dams Raid took place, and this did hit the headlines and captured the imagination of the public. Later on, the squadron was given permission by the King to have its own squadron badge and each member was presented by the Commanding Officer with a personal copy of it. J. showed me his – a small, brass lapel brooch showing one of the dams being breached, and underneath the words, *Apres moi le deluge*.

We recently visited the Bomber Command museum at Hendon in north London, which was interesting from a nostalgic point of view. We had a critical look at the one Lancaster and the one Mosquito, had a good laugh at the set piece showing the inside of a Waaf Nissen hut (so tidy and so *spacious!*), and then studied the dozens of squadron crests and emblems laid out in a large glass cabinet. Nowhere, however could we see any sign of the 617 badge. We must have overlooked it somehow, as it surely couldn't have been missed out altogether?

After leaving 617, J. spent some time with the Canadians in 6 Group, and then on to 4 Group at Marston Moor, before the war ended. These were all heavy bomber stations and did have some very tough times, losing many aircraft and many more coming back from ops badly shot up, with dead and injured on board and sometimes bombs as well, the same as we in 8 Group and all the other Groups were experiencing. It was the same story all over Bomber Command. The first priority would be for the ground crews to make the bombs safe, then put out the fires and get the injured off, and everything done at top speed in case the whole lot went up.

I suppose there must be some records in a dusty file somewhere of how often the ground crews lost the race against time and had the aircraft and bombs blow up in front of them, but as far as I can recollect this never happened at Bourn, at least not while I was there, and we were thankful to get through each busy night without catastrophes of that kind. J. was himself injured in several other incidents involving bombs, once being temporarily blinded when a marker bomb exploded almost in his face.

Sitting there in the Cathedral Close in the weak spring sunlight, trying to grasp the enormity of the events we had lived through, we gradually came to accept that these things were now in the past, and the war was really over. We were lucky and had survived, unlike so many others we had known and thousands of others all over the world. Here, we at least were on the threshold of a new life, with all its endless possibilities.

One of these possibilities made itself known to J. some time that spring. Several months previously he had applied through the usual channels for a commission in the RAF, with the idea at the back of his mind of getting back into flying. One day in April he was summoned for an interview at Group Headquarters in connection with this application, and away he went with a dispatch rider in a motorcycle and sidecar. Once there he was informed that his application was being looked upon favourably, and very shortly he could expect to hear that he was to report to Cranwell to begin his Officer Training Course.

However, J. came to the decision that enough was enough and all he wanted now was to get out of the RAF and pursue a civilian career. So he went to the commanding officer at Binbrook (who was the one who had recommended him in the first place), and said – no thanks, I want to get out. The CO was exceedingly displeased, understandably. I think it is fair to say that hard words were spoken, but I never knew exactly what was said. And I must also add that I was a trifle put out, and surprised, because it seemed to me that he was turning down a good opportunity. However, it was his decision and having made up his mind, he stuck to his guns. Before many more weeks had passed, his demobilisation came through and he was able to shake the dust of the RAF off his boots forever.

Before this happened we had one last day in Lincoln, celebrating his release by buying and eating a 4lb punnet of delicious strawberries from the market. It makes me shudder now to think of it, how we waded into those strawberries and didn't suffer any ill effects afterwards. J. says I must have eaten at least three of the pounds myself, but that's just his usual exaggeration.

Shortly afterwards, he went off to the Demob Centre and I left dismally on my last posting to Scampton. I was only there a few weeks and was so bored and anxious to be gone that I remember very little about the place. There were the usual number of new faces to get used to, but they all seem a bit vague to me now, except of course for the one face that greeted me on my arrival in the Guard Room.

My last keen memory of the Waaf is the Demob Centre itself.

Getting out didn't make such an indelible impression as going in. I knew what I was going out to and I was only concerned that there might be some hitch or delay, that I might get there and find that someone had made a mistake and I wasn't due out for another six months – such was my anxiety to be released.

The strange thing is that I can't say I was unhappy in the Service, and generally speaking I enjoyed myself, even coming to realise as time went by that it was an experience I would hate to have missed – and yet, for years afterwards I used to have nightmares about my life in uniform. Even after I was married and had children, and had travelled extensively in Africa and North America, I still used to wake up sometimes sweating in fear, convinced that I was still in the Waaf and for some mysterious reason unable to obtain my release, but was condemned to remain in the Force for the rest of my life. Gradually these dreams came less often until they stopped altogether, although I still don't know why I had them in the first place.

When I arrived at the Demob Centre, I sat around in a bare hall for what seemed like a couple of hours, with two or three hundred other Waafs, and we stared at each other without interest. Our wartime experiences were nearly at an end and I sat there thinking of all the many people I had known briefly, wondering if I should see any of them again, and remembering the many whom I knew I should never see again. I thought of Mac, and Glamour Boy Eaton-Clark, and Henry and Jimmy, and also Rosemary, presumably now living in luxury in Dallas (as promised by Hank). It's always a bit sad when a door closes – it seems so final.

However, as it happened this door was not quite closed. A Waaf crossed the room and touched me on the arm. 'Hello Joan,' she said. 'Fancy seeing you!'

It was Dulcie Barker, but a much changed Dulcie. She was now a corporal, much thinner and wearing a lot more make-up than I remembered. If she hadn't approached me first I doubt I should have recognised her, she was so different from the plump, fresh-faced girl whom I had met on the train that January morning more than three years ago. To see a familiar, friendly face in a room full of strangers was very pleasant and we were soon exchanging news. I saw that she still wore an engagement ring, but she told me very quickly that her fiancé had been a bomber pilot and he was dead, and it was *not* the same man she had been engaged to when she joined up. Evidently that had been broken off very soon after she arrived on her first station. My heart ached for her as I realised that she had joined the ranks of so many others I had known, who had watched their men fly off into the dusk, never to be heard of again. It was a sickeningly familiar story and there was not much I could say, apart from expressing regret and understanding.

Our names and numbers were called out in the next group, so we joined the slowly moving line of girls and passed through the demobilisation process almost together.

It was a disenchanting way to end my service. I went into a small room and handed my Service Pay Book to the Waaf Officer seated behind the desk, and I suppose we exchanged a few words. Then she half rose from the desk, leaned across and gave me a dead fish handshake, and with a glazed stare directed somewhere over my left shoulder, she rattled out, all in one breath and with no punctuation,
'Thankyouverymuchforallyouhavedonegoodbye.'

Just like that.

To say I was taken aback is somewhat of an understatement. I was stunned and speechless. I suppose, poor woman, she had been repeating this phrase for days on end to hundreds of us on our way out, and she would obviously have preferred us all to disappear down a big hole and relieve her of the tedium of wearing out her voice. She certainly reduced me to size. I crept out after this, my last encounter with a commissioned officer, with my hard-won confidence and self-esteem in shreds once more. What a let down!

Before I had really recovered, I found myself at the railway station, where I said goodbye to Dulcie and we went our separate ways, promising to keep in touch, as one does. As I waved her goodbye I was aware that the wheel had now turned full circle. She was the first person I met when I joined the Waaf, and the last person I saw as I left it.

I was greatly tempted to hurl my despised Waaf hat from the train window as we were speeding southwards, and I don't really know what stopped me. I sat alone in a compartment, coming to terms with the fact that I was free at last and if I wanted to put my feet up on the opposite seat or take off my tie, no one in uniform had the right to bustle in and call me Airwoman in that well-known disapproving voice. But old habits die hard and I didn't do anything of the sort, but sat there pleasantly planning my new wardrobe, with the clothing coupons and the sum of money that a grateful Government had allowed me. Only one decision was made by the time I reached London – I was going to buy nothing blue, and I was going to let my hair grow *long*.

It was a lovely day when the train steamed into Euston, back where I started from, and there at the ticket barrier J. was waiting, as arranged, and I didn't have to salute anyone any more. Life was golden and hopeful and full of promise. It was an end and a beginning.

Postscript

All the events recorded in this book took place more than forty years ago and memories are apt to play tricks on us, so it may be that I have made a few mistakes. We were discouraged, during the war, from keeping diaries, probably in case these lethal documents should fall into enemy hands, but as nearly as I can now recall it is all true. Some of the names I have changed, some I have not. And of all the people I met, I have only kept in touch with one or two from Binbrook.

For twelve years after J. and I were married we lived first in West and then East Africa, an entirely different kind of life from what had gone before. Since then we have been in England, while the children were at school, then California, and we now live in western Canada near our married daughter and her family, while our son and his family are still in England. We travel back and forth all the time between Canada and England, and my husband has been in nearly every country of the world on business. I have flown round the world once and been on Concorde.

No time in my life, however, is more clear in my mind than my years in the Waaf. Some of the people I can still visualize as if it were yesterday. That three and a half years changed my life completely and set my feet on paths which they would never have taken if the war had not occurred. 'Long ago and far away' still rings true in my memory. It was all long ago and is now far away – but, nevertheless, it happened.